Town&Country

MODERN
MANNERS

THE THINKING PERSON'S
GUIDE TO SOCIAL GRACES

EDITED BY THOMAS P. FARLEY

HEARST BOOKS
A DIVISION OF STERLING PUBLISHING CO., INC.
NEW YORK

BOOK DESIGN BY BARBARA BALCH
ILLUSTRATIONS BY CHESLEY MCLAREN

Library of Congress Cataloging-in-Publication Data
Town & Country Modern Manners: The Thinking Person's
Guide to Social Graces / edited by Thomas P. Farley.
    p. cm.
  ISBN 1-58816-454-3
 1. Etiquette. I. Farley, Thomas P.
 BJ1853.T67 2005
 395--dc22   2004027759

10 9 8 7 6 5 4 3 2 1

Published by Hearst Books
A Division of Sterling Publishing Co., Inc.
387 Park Avenue South, New York, NY 10016

Town & Country is a trademark owned by Hearst Magazines
Property, Inc., in USA, and Hearst Communications, Inc.,
in Canada. Hearst Books is a trademark owned by
Hearst Communications, Inc.

www.townandcountrymag.com

For information about custom editions, special sales, premium and
corporate purchases, please contact Sterling Special Sales
Department at 800-805-5489 or specialsales@sterlingpub.com.

Distributed in Canada by Sterling Publishing
c/o Canadian Manda Group, 165 Dufferin Street
Toronto, Ontario, Canada M6K 3H6

Distributed in Australia by Capricorn Link (Australia) Pty. Ltd.
P.O. Box 704, Windsor, NSW 2756 Australia

Manufactured in China

ISBN 1-58816-454-3

ACKNOWLEDGMENTS

REMEMBERING TO SAY THANK YOU AFTER SOMEONE extends a courtesy is perhaps the easiest of social graces. On the other hand, writing the acknowledgments for a book—let alone one called *Modern Manners*—is no simple affair. The appreciations should be short and sweet, yet comprehensive and compelling. (Full disclosure: I have a particular problem with the first adjective in the aforementioned list.)

As overseer of *Town & Country*'s popular "Social Graces" column for the past five years, I have been privileged to work with one of the most respected editors in the business. Gutsy yet glamorous, demanding yet fair, Pamela Fiori is as fine an example of social graces as you will find in magazine publishing—or anywhere else for that matter. The many members of the *Town & Country* team—past and present—who have helped make the "Social Graces" column a success include Jamie Ahn, Jennifer Bowles, John Cantrell, Linda Crowley, Rey Cruz, Stephen Dudley, Agnethe Glatved, Tracy Gold, Julie Gray, Tom Keeton, Kathleen Kent, Catherine Lowe, Monica McCollum and Linda Nardi. Those who have helped in the coordination of this anthology include Natalie Galasso, Tamar Kaplan-Marans, Anne-Marie McGintee and Rondette Amoy Smith. At Hearst Books, I'd like to thank Jacqueline Deval for her support and

Lee Fowler for her sheer enthusiasm for this project from Day One. And a special thanks goes out to Jim Brosseau, whose superb work on the first "Social Graces" anthology (published in 2002) paved the way for this one.

Modern Manners contains several years' worth of essays, by many of the finest writers of our time. My dealings with all of these individuals have been a joy, but there are two in particular who must be singled out. The effervescent and tireless Francine Maroukian possesses a passion for life and a consideration for others that is simply contagious. And Broadway and Hollywood producer David Brown, who has two essays in this collection, is a consummate gentleman if ever there was one, a man whose generous heart and considerate ways are as legendary as they are genuine. I promise not to thank my third-grade teacher, but I will thank my family, in particular my parents, Thomas and Carolyn, as well as Tara, Sean, Kevin, Lisa, Mike, Ellen, Michael and Matthew. And lastly, I'd be remiss if I left out my feisty great-aunt, the late Muriel Farley, whose forty years as a Brooklyn schoolteacher never eroded her belief in good manners and who taught me from an early age the importance of saying thank you.

Thomas P. Farley

CONTENTS

DOMESTIC TRANQUILLITY

GOING QUIETLY

INTRODUCTION

DO MANNERS REALLY MATTER IN THE TWENTY-FIRST century or are they merely a stale leftover from another era—not to be taken seriously or of any great consequence? May I offer this, to do with as you wish: not only do manners matter, but they matter greatly. Why? Because we are in danger of losing our civility, not to mention our sense of fair play, our consideration of the feelings of others, and our regard for all those seemingly small gestures (call them niceties, if you must) that ease our path through an increasingly complicated and cumbersome post–September 11 world.

When *Town & Country* began its life back in 1846, well-behaved people were few and far between, but those who were probably did read *Town & Country*. As time went on and as education became more available, behavior improved—not for superficial reasons but for practical ones: a well-mannered person had an easier time of it, often getting what he or she wanted faster and more effectively than the one who was rude and demanding.

This remains true to this day. The problem is that good manners and polite people are scarce, outnumbered by boors and bullies who manage to get their way by pushing and shoving, ranting and raving and making a fuss.

But we at *Town & Country* say enough is enough—hence the second volume of essays from our popular column called "Social Graces." The first volume, published in 2002, did so well, that there has been demand for another (maybe there's hope after all). This latest batch of essays delves into such subjects as Andy Rooney's take on the abuses of Christmas-card sending; the modern problem of dealing with your children's nanny; and David Brown's persuasive plea for civility. Other topics range from the art of listening to elevator etiquette (yes, there really is such a thing).

These are not lectures but, rather, musings—thinking aloud, if you will—about modern behavior. Is it that we are less demanding of ourselves and our children? Does our often-hurried state or the availability of electronic, time-saving devices—e-mail, cell phones, Blackberries—reduce us to blunt messages or, worse, cut us off entirely from each other? And, if so, what can we do about it?

While we may never return to the days of the well-composed, error-free, handwritten letter, we could, let's face it, be a lot more tactful in what we say and how we say it. And in the long run, when did losing one's temper ever gain anything?

Let's put immediate gratification aside and think of the consequences, starting here and now, with this handy little volume filled with eloquent words of advice well worth following. Give it to a friend in need or keep it for yourself as a reminder of just how little effort it takes to go a long, long way in this life. And if you like what you read, there's no need to go on and on about it. A simple "thank you" will do.

Pamela Fiori
Editor in chief
Town & Country

EVERYDAY
COURTESIES

I
TRY A LITTLE
TENDERNESS

The Return of Gallantry

by Jill Kargman

The modern male may not resemble a knight in shining armor, but increasingly, he is behaving like one.

In 1999, when I was still single, my love life was more *Les Misérables* than *Sex and the City*. I felt I could not swing a sequined baguette without hitting a Dutch-treating, non-door-opening, unchivalrous buffoon. But thank the stars above, in a postmillennial ray of light, times have changed (hurray!). I don't know if it's simply the mood of the nation (at a point when everyone is feeling more sensitive all around), but after a decades-long absence, gallantry is truly back.

Of course, for the longest time, gallantry—a code that encompasses bravery, gentlemanliness and politeness—was sorely missing from American culture. Once, when I was a child, my mother was laden with shopping bags on the subway, and not a chap on the train offered his seat. In elevators, men often stormed out instead of letting women off first. On street corners, they would dart in front of you and steal your cab.

The outlook on the dating scene was no better. In the mid-nineties, a friend of mine was set up with a man who wanted her to pick him up at his place. She entered the featureless white-brick horror show of an apartment (filled with bachelor-pad no-nos such as framed beer posters and black leather sectionals) and noticed his kitchen sink, which was overflowing with coated plates, encrusted utensils and glasses brimming with stinky brown water. He looked at her, smiled, and pointed to the neglected pile: "No wife," he grunted. Taxi!

My friend Dana recalls the time that her date stopped at a teller machine to withdraw some cash. When the ATM spat out his receipt, which showed his six-figure balance, he shoved it in her face and said, "Not bad, eh?" Check, please!

All of these disturbing anecdotes made us wonder: who raised these people? Well, in fairness to the moms, maybe we damsels have been a little schizo. First we wanted the dashing gestures, the affection and the caretaking. But then feminism arrived. We wanted equal pay (naturally), and some women weren't so sure that they wanted a door held for them anymore. Somehow, the independence we craved served to cripple gallantry, and men were left confused. "Do I hold the door?" gents wondered. "Or will she feel patronized?"

Lately, though, good manners seem to have returned: the neotraditionalist daughters of feminists are inviting back the chivalrous codes of yesteryear, and men are catching on. Now in a crowded store, men are gesturing for women to go ahead of them. The other day, I saw a father teaching his son to allow a group of women to pass through a door first.

Why is gallantry so much on the rise? First of all, even before Americans banded together in September 2001, the whole New Economy was spearheaded by a different breed of male. In a plot twist that could have been lifted from *Revenge of the Nerds,* cocky, jockish, butt-pinching Wall Streeters were trumped by sensitive tech types who never got noticed by women when they were younger. In the late 1990s, when the former outcasts became successful businessmen, they finally got the female attention that they had craved all along. And when they did, they showered those women with kindness.

Not that we need to be hailed, but being treated well and getting respect is a welcome change. Women have finally realized that there is enough danger in our society; we don't want to invite more by taking up with a bad boy.

For guys who have yet to catch on, listen up: we're merely looking for small gestures; it's not about saving us from the fire swamp, as in *The Princess Bride*. Just the other day, for example, I was walking into the Metropolitan Museum of Art, and those massive doors, which usually thrust me backward onto the street, were held open by the man in front of me. And I didn't feel patronized; I was grateful.

"Men somehow figured out all those details," Dana says, "like putting us in the cab and then walking around to the other side so we don't have to slide." Modern manners also include not leaving cell phones on the table (rude), answering them mid-dinner (abominable) or taking a call from another woman during the meal (downright slimy!).

And speaking of dinner, after years of men and women's splitting everything down the middle, it also seems that men are once again insisting on footing the bill. "I remember just a few years back, I'd do the mock reach-for-the-wallet at the end of a meal," my friend Caroline recalls, "and my dates would actually let me split the check with them! That never happens anymore."

As a working woman, however, I also feel that there is such

a thing as too much "taking care of," and if for every little movie ticket and popcorn and cab ride the man is whipping out his wallet, you can start to feel like a kept woman. It is, like many things, a delicate balance. When a man insists on paying for dinner, we need to step up and pay for the theater tickets or the drinks.

After all, our mothers and grandmothers fought hard for equal rights. We don't want a full-fledged return to the Arthurian court's male-centric code. Instead of their carrying a sword, we'd love it if our men would simply carry the plane tickets and offer to help us with our luggage. "I'm even seeing a difference at the gym," says Dana. "Now if a man spots you walking to use a machine that he is heading toward, he'll step back and even help you get set up." It seems our knights have a little less armor on their hearts.

> For guys who have yet to catch on, listen up: we're merely looking for small gestures; it's not about saving us from the fire swamp.

The return of the gallant man has been mirrored (and perhaps partly inspired) by our popular culture. In the film *Kate & Leopold*, twenty-first-century advertising executive Meg Ryan falls for the charming nineteenth-century suitor played by Hugh Jackman. In *Bridget Jones' Diary*, the good guy portrayed by Colin Firth ultimately triumphs over the user played by Hugh Grant and wins the heart of Renée Zellweger. Even the ever-gallant Superman has made a comeback in the television series *Smallville*, which chronicles the polite superhero's early years.

It has been said that men are the new women, and in an era of male facials, self-expression, attention to style and getting in shape, it could be true. But perhaps the role reversal has come about more because women like the ones in *Sex and the City* feel so empowered—sexually and otherwise—that now men are the ones who often want to take things slow.

But this new, measured pace of courtship hasn't stopped men from showing they care. One male friend of mine was dating his girlfriend for only two months when she had to leave on a week-long business trip. She called him the first night, saying how cold it was, and the next day she received an overnight package containing a cashmere scarf. Moves such as that were unusual just a few years ago, because people were terrified of scaring the other person off. It was as if a simple act of genuine thoughtfulness meant "I worship you" and "This is the beginning of lots of smothering." Luckily, however, fears like that have subsided. As new fears have taken the larger stage, we look differently at how we need to relate to and connect with one another.

Chivalrous firemen became overnight heartthrobs, and police officers, today's knights, are modern-day heroes. Even civilians seem more courageous in daily life. The world's turmoil is decidedly not a good thing, but at least there's a bumper crop in gallantry. And while we damsels are beyond thrilled to bid adieu to boorish men, we are even more ecstatic to have real partners who truly make us feel like women. Memo to men: Nice guys finish first.

Win Some, Lose Some

by Charles Osgood

The victor may get the spoils, but the true rewards
go to those who are good sports.

We all have little victories and defeats in our lives, and some big ones, too. Rare is the day that we don't add to both our "Win" and "Loss" columns. Obviously we would like the Ws to outweigh the Ls, but our appetite for victory and our aversion to defeat seem to have sharpened in recent years. We don't handle either one very well anymore.

The role models we get from the worlds of entertainment, sports and politics have not been terribly helpful. You'd think that these public individuals, who must deal with winning and losing on a regular basis, would set a sportsmanlike example for the rest of us.

Whatever happened to the old gladiator mantra "We who are about to die salute you?" It gets me to thinking about that Joe Raposo song "(Here's to the) Winners." Is it any surprise that he never bothered to write a song called "Here's to the Losers"? (Truth be told, someone else did.)

It feels wonderful to win, but how should winners express

their satisfaction in the moment of victory? How should they comport themselves in the presence of those they've vanquished? As if they had just conquered Nazi Germany or found a cure for cancer? Conversely, how should the losers express their frustration and disappointment in moments of defeat? A sense of perspective is difficult to come by in hard-fought contests.

For their part, today's sports fans haven't come that far from the days of the gladiator. They know that their teams can't win 'em all, but they do want to see the thrill of victory and the agony of defeat acted out. And so the players, who are also players in the theatrical sense, celebrate not only game victories but completely routine plays as well. You'll see some NFL players doing a little dance to taunt the opposition every time they catch a pass or make a tackle. It's a far cry from the days when Tom Landry of the Dallas Cowboys would tell Hollywood Henderson to try to look as if he'd done it before. Landry himself used to stand stoically on the sidelines like a man waiting for a bus. You could not tell from his facial expression or bearing whether his team was ahead or behind.

> Victory is better than defeat, just as surely as health, wealth and wisdom are better than sickness, poverty and ignorance.

In the poem "If," his famous litany of what it takes to "be a man, my son," Rudyard Kipling observes, "If you can meet with triumph and disaster, / And treat those two impostors just the same. . . ." They *are* impostors, you know. A musician friend of mine has a sign on his studio wall that reads SHOW ME A GOOD

LOSER AND I'LL SHOW YOU A LOSER! Do musicians think in terms of winners and losers, too? Are they that competitive? Many of them are. For in the arts, as in virtually every kind of human endeavor, there is an element of competition.

There's a story, apocryphal perhaps, about Fritz Kreisler, the virtuoso violinist, sitting in the audience at a Berlin Philharmonic concert next to pianist Josef Hofmann. The twelve-year-old prodigy Jascha Heifetz was performing a solo in Tchaikovsky's Violin Concerto in D Major.

"It's very hot in here, isn't it?" Kreisler is supposed to have whispered to Hofmann between movements.

Without a moment's hesitation, Hofmann is said to have whispered back, "Not for pianists."

Artists may not like to admit it, but in the arts, as in virtually every endeavor, there is an element of competition. It's human nature to want to do better than somebody else. Victory is better than defeat, just as surely as health, wealth and wisdom are better than sickness, poverty and ignorance. With winning comes not only the thrill of victory but also the gold medal, the job, the Oscar, the Nobel, the presidency or the Lombardi Trophy—the prize that goes to the winner of the Super Bowl.

That coveted award is named for Vince Lombardi, the legendary football coach often credited (if "credit" is the appropriate word here) with saying "Winning isn't everything. It's the only thing!" In fact, he never said it. It may have been another coach, UCLA's Red Sanders, who uttered those words.

While he was in college, Lombardi was one of Fordham University's "Seven Blocks of Granite." (Fordham is my alma mater.) After graduation, he taught Latin and chemistry and coached at St. Cecilia High School (also my alma mater) in Englewood, New Jersey. What he said, according to people there who knew him well, was "Winning isn't everything, but wanting to win is."

Later, as a coach for the Green Bay Packers, he pushed his players to work hard. And you bet he wanted to imbue them with a strong desire to win—but not at all costs. That would have been inconsistent with character. And to Lombardi, character was what counted most—on the field and in life.

In the end, we do seem to save our respect for the individuals who show the most character when faced with situations of triumph or loss. We admire people like Joe DiMaggio, Jacqueline Kennedy, Billie Jean King, Michael Jordan and Christopher Reeve—a partial list, but you get the idea.

I recently took my seventeen-year-old son, Jamie, a high school senior, to the campus of a college to which he was applying on an early-decision basis. I waited with other parents as our children went in for their interviews. In most cases, as each one emerged, you could tell right away whether the outcome was a W or an L. Some of the kids came running out grinning and with thumbs up. Others came out looking crushed or in tears. A few parents of the latter seemed angry and berated their offspring for not having done well enough. When Jamie came through the door, I caught his eye across the room, and he smiled. I swear there was no way to tell from his face or manner how things had gone. I could not have been more proud.

One Hundred Thousand Welcomes

by Frank McCourt

Its green fields are legendary. So is the stout. Yet what makes Ireland truly special is the warmth of its people.

If you're Irish, come into the parlour,
There's a welcome there for you,
And if your name is Timothy or Pat
So long as you come from Ireland
There's a welcome on the mat;
If you come from the Mountains of Mourne,
Or Killarney's lakes so blue,
We'll sing you a song and we'll make a fuss,
Whoever you are you're one of us,
If you're Irish this is the place for you.

—from "If You're Irish, Come into the Parlour"
by Shaun Glenville and Frank Miller

I f you're Irish and you look at the proliferation of Irish pubs worldwide, you're comforted by the thought that you need never be lonely again anywhere on earth. Indeed, you can ignore what the song says: it doesn't matter if your name is Timothy or Pat or if you come from the Mountains of Mourne. There's a place for you in the huge Irish pubs of Berlin, Madrid, Paris and Sydney, not to mention in Ireland itself. They're all trying to capture that elusive but magical quality we call Irish hospitality. As wannabes the world over strive to match that warmth, that welcome, in Ireland it just comes naturally.

I'm Irish myself, and the bit of education I have helps me understand the traditional hospitality of the Irish. Sometimes it seems they're simply good at it—welcoming the stranger, making him or her feel at home. You see it when you deplane at Shannon or Dublin: "Here, let me help you with that bag, that door; and mind your head getting into the car; and isn't it a grand day, thank God; and if you're worn out from your flight, we'll have you in your bed in no time."

From the small, family-run bed-and-breakfast houses to the five-star hotels, there is a sense of immediate ease that is hard to find elsewhere in the world. There is a welcome on the mat, and it says *Céad Míle Fáilte* (pronounced KAID MEE-la FALL-che)—Irish for "one hundred thousand welcomes."

Americans return from there and tell me what a friendly country Ireland is. Certainly one of the things that appeals to them is the common language, not having to parlez-vous their way around the country. Ah, you'll say, "But they speak English throughout the British Isles." And the Irish will say back to you, "Yes, indeed, but an English of inferior quality." What American wanderer hasn't returned shaking a head over the other accents: Scottish, Welsh, Cornish or Cockney? It may be a stereotype or it may be a simple statement of fact that the Irish in Ireland are hospitable. Even if I accept my own flat declaration that they're "good at it," I wonder why and, in wonder, return to my childhood and the example of my mother.

Whenever there was a knock at the door, we looked at our mother to see what we should do. If it was a Monday or a Thursday, she would shake her head and signal silence, for these were rent-man days or insurance-man days, and when you didn't have the money, you ignored the knock.

This "silent treatment" went against my mother's nature. You would never ignore a knock at the door; it might be the Holy Family looking for shelter or a cup of tea. That was half a joke but you never knew. And if it wasn't the Holy Family, it could be any poor family or simply a single wandering beggar.

In the Limerick of my youth, during the 1940s, there was no shortage of beggars. My parents, with their sense of history or at least their feeling for it, understood the long, dark aftermath of the Great Famine one hundred years before. In the lanes of the city, where books were scarce, Famine stories never faded, stories so terrible they were often whispered.

Any beggar at the door was knocking for history, reminding us that his or her ancestors once had roofs over their heads and kettles whistling on the hob, and surely we could spare a cut of bread and a jam jar of tea.

Even in the worst of times, my mother, Angela, would bring beggars to our table while we watched and wondered at the way she could take half a loaf and perform a "loaves and fishes" with it or the way she stretched the tea leaves for three till there was enough to fill the jam jars for six people: herself, the beggar, my brothers—Alphie, Michael and Malachy—and me.

There were times we grumbled there wasn't enough and we were still hungry, and that is when she would invoke the Holy Family or the Great Famine. She knew it was hard to be giving away the little bit you had left, but you had to put yourself in the place of the beggar who took no pleasure knocking on people's doors, the beggar who knew there was more hope of a morsel in the lanes of the poor than in the grand streets of the comfortable.

You were not to turn anyone from your door, because there was great shame in such an act, shame for the one hiding behind the door. In olden Ireland, we were told, all doors were open to everyone, but then the Famine came, and the roads were clogged with the starving, the diseased, the destitute, dragging themselves desperately from door to door, and my mother knew from the stories handed down that if you had a few healthy potatoes, you had to feed your own. Ignoring the knock became a common thing in Famine times and the cause of a great sadness that could not be helped.

> As wannabes the world over strive to match that warmth, that welcome, in Ireland it just comes naturally.

In his 1972 book, *The Mountain People*, anthropologist Colin Turnbull wrote of the Ik, a tribe in Uganda whose existence was threatened by famine. Abandoning their previously humane ways, the Ik espoused an individualistic lifestyle as part of their new means of survival. Turnbull describes how the tribe's personality changed from being open, generous and good-humored to quarrelsome, petty and cruel. They became so insensitive that they even laughed over a toddler crawling toward a fire who was about to be burned. The Famine surely had a similar effect on the Irish, dampening their spirit of generosity and hospitality.

But that spirit is back full force, and so is the fun, the *craic,* as they say in Ireland. There are smiles in Ireland now where the teeth are white, polished and all there. (In my day and in my lane a smile was a glimpse of a Welsh coal mine.) These days, Ireland is said to have the fastest-growing economy in all of Europe. They even call it the Celtic Tiger. And the country has one of the youngest populations in Europe—with 40 percent of her people being under the age of twenty-five. Those young men and women are not as tormented by history as my generation once was, and they've crawled out from under centuries of political oppression and church dogma.

Pity my mother died in 1981 and didn't see the New Ireland, the Celtic Tiger. Pity she couldn't see the world flocking to her country for the *craic* and the *seisiúns,* traditional Irish music played in the pubs. She was never an enthusiast of drinking establishments, but if that's where the singing was, that's where she'd be— and she could enjoy a whole night on a glass of ginger ale. For her generation, and even for mine, a going or a coming was an event that required the ritual of hospitality. Sit down there now, and I'll make you a nice cup of tea.

For the pint or the noggin, you repair to the pub, but if you want to get inside Ireland, stay there in the sitting room with the tea, the cousin you're visiting or the lady who runs your bed-and-breakfast.

If there's one thing we could all learn from the Irish, it would be to enjoy life, not rush it. God knows there's no hurry, but if there were, the world would wait.

That's what my mother would have said to anyone.

II

PEACEFUL
COEXISTENCE

Have a Little Patience

by M. J. Ryan

For a change, *T&C* takes its finger *off* the pulse
and explores the joy of accepting life as it comes.

Not so long ago, while boarding a flight with open seating, I was brusquely shoved by the woman behind me, a traveler apparently incapable of waiting thirty seconds before finding her own seat. "Now that's *rude*," I thought.

The more I considered her act, however, the more I was able to identify with her. We are in constant motion these days and expect everything and everyone around us to go even faster. As David Shenk, author of *The End of Patience,* notes, thanks to such advances as voice-activated speed dialing, DSL and instant messaging—not to mention older yet no less ubiquitous conveniences like overnight mail and fax machines—"Quickness has disappeared. We now experience only degrees of slowness."

The result of all this rushing is that many of us suffer from chronic impatience. I was no exception. I couldn't stand how slowly my computer booted up. I would push the elevator call button more than once, just to make it arrive faster. (It doesn't help.) And I typically used the one-minute cook option on my microwave because it was quicker than punching in the time.

Then, one day, I was in a copy shop where I got caught waiting in line behind two very old women who were carefully counting coins to pay for their copies. I fumed inside and eventually ripped out a dollar bill for my forty-cent purchase, pitched it over their white heads, and stormed out of the store. It was only after I drove away that it struck me how abysmally I had behaved. It wasn't a matter of life or death that I got out of the shop so quickly. Sure, I was busy, but a few seconds more would not have ruined my day.

I think that was the point when I finally stopped and asked myself why I was always hurrying. Was I enjoying my life? Was I being as nice to others as I should? Was rushing around actually getting me anywhere? The more I thought about it, the more I realized that I was mildly irritated all of the time and was in fact quite snippy when things didn't go my way. Was this any way to live?

Indeed, as a society, the faster things go, the less patience we are able to muster. This is a problem because no matter how much we prepare for life's little annoyances, they still throw us for a loop. When we can least afford to wait, we seem to encounter grocery lines, traffic jams and automated message systems, not to mention hour-long delays at airport security, where removing our shoes and belts has become the norm.

Our lack of patience creates even greater problems when the roadblocks are more than mere annoyances. How do we handle illnesses, relationship conflicts, job crises or parenting problems? Such situations can require a painful amount of patience. Yet we must be ready to let go and allow the passage of time to work its magic whether we are convalescing from heart surgery or mending a broken heart. Rushing to get our lives back to normal before it is time can have disastrous consequences.

Patience greases the gears of our lives and our relationships by giving us the ability to pause and decide on the best response. Consequently, it helps us be more polite to strangers, more loving toward our families and better able to get what we truly want.

Patience also enables us to graciously accept the obstacles life places in our path and to respond with courtesy, courage and optimism. This doesn't mean that we should like the curveballs that are hurled at us, but we can at least recognize that they are part and parcel of being alive. So rather than whine or complain, we roll up our sleeves and tackle the tasks at hand while treating others kindly in the process.

As a society, the faster things go, the less patience we are able to muster.

We can all agree on the merits of being patient. In fact, I have no doubt that at one time or another, somebody told us that we should be more patient. Maybe we've even said it to ourselves. Most likely, however, it didn't happen. Simply saying we should do something, then beating ourselves up when we don't, only fosters guilt and shame, so I'm not going to advocate you do that. Rather, I'm going to offer some suggestions.

- Have you reached the limit of your tolerance with someone at work or at home? Take a vigorous walk. You'll burn off the stress hormones that accumulate in your system and will be better able to reengage your good humor when you return.

- Ask yourself: What's the worst thing that could happen if . . . I'm late / the deal doesn't come through / what I want doesn't happen in the time frame I've set? Can I survive that? Most likely you can.

- Put a pebble in your pocket. In an irritating situation, move the pebble from one pocket to the other. This will interrupt the impatience cycle and give you a chance to regroup.

- If you are standing on a line, take yourself on a mental vacation. Visualize the most peaceful place you can conjure and then imagine yourself there. Bring to mind the feelings that such a place evokes in you. Rather than focus on how long you have to wait, relish this chance to take a little daydream trip to Tahiti or the Alps.

- Celebrate small milestones on the way to the completion of a large project. Ten pages done? Take yourself to lunch. When we stop to take satisfaction breaks, we give ourselves the resilience to press on.

- Try a "traffic light" meditation. While sitting at a red light, take three consecutive breaths. Simply notice how each breath goes in and comes out.

- The old advice of counting to ten in a heated situation works. It gives you a chance to remember what really matters to you: blowing off steam or finding an effective solution. If ten doesn't work, try twenty.

- Ask for help. Often we are impatient because we are over-loaded. There's no prize at the end of your life for doing too much, particularly if it's done while you're frazzled.

Once you've started down the road to becoming more

patient, ask yourself: Am I more relaxed, even when I have to wait? Am I more pleasant to be around? More resilient? If so, use your newfound patience to keep at it.

Recently my six-year-old and I were stuck for three hours on San Francisco's Bay Bridge. In the past, I would have fussed and fumed the whole time, making myself and everyone around me miserable. But I decided to make the best of it. We told stories, sang along with the radio and chatted with fellow strandees. Would I have rather been home? Of course. But with patience, the experience was as pleasant as could be. And my daughter complained only once.

Elevator Ups and Downs

by Patricia Marx

*The next time you take a ride,
make sure your manners rise to the occasion.*

H ere are a few things you should never utter in an elevator: "The doctor says I'll be contagious for three more days." "What do you mean, the safety brakes don't always work?" "I think I'm going to be sick, and I'm not sure I can hold it." And, of course, don't ever shout "Fire!" in a crowded elevator. But that's obvious.

Indeed, most of the basics of elevator etiquette are obvious, since they derive from the existential predicament of being trapped in a very small space with total strangers. It's a situation somewhat like the one described in Jean-Paul Sartre's play *No Exit,* in which three characters find themselves impounded together in a room. "Where are the instruments of torture . . . the racks and red-hot pincers and all the other paraphernalia?" one of them asks. He soon discovers that, in the words of one of his new roommates, "hell is other people." And that hell goes on and on and on, perhaps forever.

Fortunately, hell in an elevator is short-lived. Well, usually it is. I can remember one ride that seemed to last for years. I was traveling with a friend who asked me if it was my birthday. When I answered in the affirmative, everyone in the car burst into song.

Another time I almost drowned in a Manhattan town house when the elevator I was in screeched to a halt a few inches below the basement floor, made a loud humming noise and quickly filled with water infused with cigarette butts, cockroaches and worse. I couldn't open the door, nor could I get the elevator to move. By the time I reached the police on the phone, the water had risen to the top of my thighs. Eventually, rescuers arrived, but not until after I had shimmied up the cables to the first floor, where I tried to no avail to get the door to open. (Years later, while watching *Die Hard*, I learned that there is a safety lever you can push to exit.)

But those instances are exceptions. The majority of elevator rides do not feature a spirited group of people singing "Happy Birthday," nor situations in which a lone individual is confronted with a mechanical meltdown. More typically, you will find yourself accompanied by others who follow the well-established rules of politesse. If everyone acts appropriately, the strangers you share this space with remain strangers for the duration of the ride. At least, that is the goal.

Hence, passengers face the elevator door to minimize awkward eye contact. If you must look at something and have no interest in gazing at your shoes, set your eyes on the panel that indicates which floor the elevator is currently on.

Personal space is at a premium on an elevator and must be respected. Accordingly, pets, bicycles and large packages do not have the same rights of occupancy as people; if the elevator is crowded, they should be taken in the freight car. If there isn't one, people with large or living objects should wait for the next elevator.

For similar reasons, strollers must be folded. In fact, if you have a baby, fold him or her up, or at least activate the little one's mute button. While you're at it, hit your own mute button. Although some people may not mind being told by a stranger to have a nice day, I enjoy not having a nice day once in a while and find the expression bossy and intrusive. In any case, do not carry on loud conversations, especially those having to do with personal matters or work issues (unless what you have to say is very spicy—and I'll be the judge of that). Certainly, there shouldn't be any talking on cell phones, as this will infringe on the privacy of those who do not want to be disabused of their illusions that they are alone in the first-class cabin of an ocean liner. To hush a noisy passenger, look worried and ask that everyone be silent so you can listen for whether there is a problem with the elevator's motor.

> Personal space is at a premium on an elevator and must be respected.

Needless to say, you should not eat in an elevator. If you insist, you may discreetly drink a soda. But use a straw, please. And if you spill anything on me, you'd better pay for the dry cleaning.

Of course, a discussion of elevator etiquette cannot be restricted to what goes on in the tiny cubicle. There is also the getting on and off to consider. Let's start with the waiting. It is rude as well as moronic to press the elevator call button incessantly. Bear in mind the possibility that by your being such a nag, the elevator might decide to teach you a lesson and take an extra-long time getting to your floor.

Once the elevator has deigned to arrive, step on as quickly as you can without plowing anyone down in the process. Men should allow women to enter and exit first only when no fancy choreography is required. In other words, a man standing next to the elevator door should not jostle his way to the rear so that the woman standing in the back can get out before he does. You should not cram yourself onto a jam-packed elevator unless beckoned to do so either by the passengers or your wailing six-year-old who is already aboard and appears especially afraid of becoming an orphan.

Don't stand in the open doorway while finishing up a conversation with a friend who's talking to you from the hall. And certainly don't hold the elevator for someone who is "just getting her coat" and will be there "in a sec." Elevators are not like Halley's comet; they come with great frequency unless someone—and I think you know whom I mean—holds them up. So if you or your friend are not ready for takeoff, wait for the next elevator.

One last rule: Actually, it is not mine but that of the humorist Robert Benchley. If you are in an elevator attended by an operator, do not ask him or her what the weather is like. As Benchley pointed out, the elevator operator spends the entire day in the elevator and is absolutely the last person who has any idea of whether it seems like rain is on the way. You may ask if the couple in 8G is getting divorced, but don't ask how it looks outside. And yet, that is probably the most frequently asked question of an elevator operator.

Don't Do This in Public

by Patricia Volk

Annoying habits that belong behind closed doors.

The first time I saw somebody do something repulsive in public, I was in a car. So was he. We'd both pulled up to a light. The man was picking his nose. Did he think, because he was in a car, nobody could see him? Do people do horrible things out in the open because they're so used to being alone, they forget they're not?

The computer has something to do with it. A woman files her nails in front of her laptop, so she files them on line at the movies. I used to work with a man who publicly self-manicured with a shiny nail clipper. Crisp clicks accompanied parings that flew through the air. I silently prayed that the projectiles wouldn't take out an eye.

Restaurants bring out the worst in people. Lipstick at the table is bad enough. (Why should anyone have to observe you smacking your lips as you apply your Coral Belize?) Preening doesn't belong in public. It's too intimate. It floors the brakes on conversation. Chanel No. 5 perfume is dandy but not spritzed over my tarte tatin. And face powder? There's food below. Stuff snows off the puff. You don't know that?

Cole Porter set his table with a gold toothpick at every spot.

(And you thought he played the piano after supper.) My mother's most elegant friend, Harriet, is the proud owner of a solid-gold toothpick that she keeps in a padded red leather case. Harriet makes an elaborate ritual out of picking her teeth, as if it's okay because the toothpick is made of a precious metal. That does not, in fact, make it any less offensive than if it were wood or plastic. But the worst is my dear friend who suffers from compromised bridgework. "I know this is terrible," Beverly laughs, fishing for her floss. At least she doesn't do all thirty-two. I can understand how awful it must be to have confit trapped between your bicuspids. That's the second-best reason ladies' rooms were invented.

Strangers have no right to co-opt your brain cells. I never again want to be hostage to someone's phone conversation in a public place. On the other hand, "in public" does not necessarily mean physically in front of others. Now that cell phones enable mobility, some friends conduct conversations from the bathroom. To Whom It May Concern: flushing is audible. So are other things. A simple rule: If you normally do it in the bathroom, don't share it.

To the filmmaker I had dinner with who blew his nose in the restaurant's linen napkin, I want you to know that I will never, ever invite you to my home. I will never eat at that restaurant again either. What if I got your napkin? And what about the busboy who cleared? Was he wearing rubber gloves?

Speaking of rubber gloves, the people at my local gourmet grocery store must wear them by law. But please, I'd like to know, if you scratch your head and then catch falling slices of apple-smoked turkey breast with that same hand, do you really think I'm going to eat it? Has it occurred to you that's exactly why so many freshly cut packages of meat and cheese are left behind instead of being brought to the checkout line? I wish I could tell you not to scratch your head before you touch my honey ham, but I can't. I can, however, mention it to your manager.

Here's something terrible that's only getting worse: theater- and moviegoers who chat during the action or, worse, loudly predict the outcome. They speak up as if they're vying to be the first in class to blurt out "I bet she's going to lock the door when he goes down to the cellar." Or "You watch. He's going to fall in love with her friend from the laundromat." I turn in my seat and say "Please!" or *"Shush."* When that doesn't work, I even say, beseechingly, "You're ruining it for me." The transgressors look back at me, invariably shocked. Perhaps they thought they were at home, sitting on the sofa in front of their television.

> Do people do horrible things out in the open because they're so used to being alone, they forget they're not?

And then there's name-dropping. I suppose the real unpleasantness I experience in the company of people who practice this habit comes from how sad I feel for them. Name-dropping is a desperate and obvious attempt to impress the person you're with. That said, I should feel flattered when people name-drop because it means they're trying to impress me. But it's as wearisome as any exposure to raw neediness is. Interesting how the worst name-droppers are the people who tell you how much they loathe name-dropping, as in: "Henry Kissinger and Nan Kempner both told me they can't stand name-droppers, and frankly, I couldn't agree more."

It would be counterproductive to ask someone to lower his boom box when it's turned up to DEAFEN precisely because its owner wants to impose his music on you. Cuticle gnawing, trichotillomania, California hair flinging and leg pumping are nervous tics and fall into a separate category. They're compulsions. Who am I to tell you to stop? So I walk away or study my shoes. Correcting something a person has no control over would hurt his or her feelings. Good manners are based on being concerned about how the other person feels. They're the cornerstone of civilization. The late C. Z. Guest knew that. Her generation even had a word for it. It's a word that's gone the way of "How may I help you?" and "Would you be so kind?" and "I beg your pardon." It's a word you almost never hear anymore: *decorum.*

When Bad Things Happen to Bad People

by Jeff Marx and Robert Lopez

Don't feel too guilty for laughing.
In all likelihood, they had it coming.

T he "social graces" term of the month is Schadenfreude, a word brought to us by the Germans, meaning "taking pleasure in the misfortune of others." Have you ever said mockingly, "It couldn't have happened to a nicer guy" about someone you didn't care for very much? So have we. Have you ever been in a restaurant and seen someone jump because he or she spotted an insect on the table? There's nothing like it! We wouldn't wish it on ourselves, but when it happens to someone else—especially someone dislikable—we just can't help it: a part of us wants to laugh.

There's an entire song about Schadenfreude in our Broadway musical, *Avenue Q*. To our knowledge, it's the only song ever written on the subject—which is probably why we were invited to write this column. To create the song, we had to research the topic exhaustively. At long last, we decided to put the lyrics in the mouth of Gary Coleman, one of the characters in our show. (You remember Gary Coleman—the child actor who won hearts in the late 1970s in the hit series *Diff'rent Strokes*?) Well, in *Avenue Q,* it's not the actual actor—it's a woman playing the role. The real Gary became rich and famous overnight, but his star fell hard. After suing his parents for pocketing his fortune, working as a security guard, famously punching out a female autograph seeker and, more recently, running for governor of California, he's become the butt of jokes.

In short, it hasn't been easy for poor Gary. If he looked at the ridicule objectively, he'd realize that people just enjoy seeing the really high fall really low. Did he deserve his fall from grace? (For that matter, did he deserve his rise to fame?) Fortunately, he's able to poke fun at himself, too. And he acknowledges that it's okay to laugh at other people's misfortunes.

> We wouldn't wish it on ourselves, but when it happens to someone else—especially someone dislikable—we just can't help it: a part of us wants to laugh.

If their main characters didn't have to suffer, we probably wouldn't enjoy plays and movies as much as we do. Without the pretend problems of pretend people, there would be no drama. And without drama, there would be no entertainment. And without entertainment, there's no fun. So, let's do the math. Suffering—as long as it's not your own—is fun!

It's a very quick ethical leap from fiction to reality. Just start by turning on your television. *The People's Court, Divorce Court* and *Judge Judy* are old favorites. Now there's *Survivor, Fear Factor* and *The Amazing Race.* Witness one of the most popular catchphrases of the day: "You're fired." When we watch a reality show, we are peering in on real people's problems and deriving amusement and delight from them.

And what about the Miss America pageant? Is it all about rooting for someone to win? Or does part of the enjoyment come from watching someone come this close and leave empty-handed? How about *American Idol*? You don't feel happy when a certain contestant gets cut? Oh, please. Yes, you do. It's a harmless pleasure. The off-key crooners won't ever know about your mockery.

But not all mishaps lead to this kind of gratification. Beheadings don't qualify. Nor do car accidents. The serious stuff doesn't make anybody happy. Death doesn't usually make anyone smile. Neither does seeing a restaurant patron choking on a bone at the next table.

We've sort of become modern-day Solomons on the subject, able to evaluate whether someone's mishap is worthy of our joy. Here are some examples, to help you discern for yourself.

Your boss gets jury duty: Is this a cause for celebration? *Yes.*

Your boss, presumably, has made your life miserable in the past and therefore has it coming.

Your best friend gets indicted: *No.*

You are supposed to love your best friend. If you're a good person, you won't be happy at this unfortunate turn of events.

The straight-A student in your class messes up on a pop quiz and gets a B+: *Yes.*

The anguished expression and trembling lower lip of your anal-retentive classmate should be enough to keep you smiling through lunch. Even if you got a lower grade, you are entitled to some satisfaction here, because straight-A students need to learn they aren't perfect.

The presidential candidate you opposed wins the election, then leads the nation into unprecedented disaster and his approval ratings go way down: *No*.

As tempting as it may be to say "I told you so," any national disaster presumably affects us all, and there is no room for gloating.

A pregnant woman on crutches misses her train: *No*.

We feel bad for even coming up with this example.

A Broadway show created by two talented young composers wins three Tony Awards. During one of their acceptance speeches, they go over the allotted time and are drowned out by the play-off music: *Yes*.

This happened to us. Bobby was so unnerved by the happy, jazzy music that he omitted mentioning his wife's name. It's okay—you may feel free to feel good.

Perhaps Leona Helmsley, the so-called Queen of Mean, gets caught cheating on her taxes (again): *Yes*.

It is (hypothetically) discovered that the late Mr. Rogers was guilty of the same crime: *No*.

In fact, if Fred Rogers cheated on his taxes, we'd be glad that he got away with it. We love Mr. Rogers.

It's not okay to feel Schadenfreude about people you like. It's not okay to feel it about the poor and/or virtuous. It is okay to feel Schadenfreude about people you dislike or don't care about. It is okay to feel it about the privileged and/or unscrupulous. And the beauty of it is that they'll never be aware of how much amusement they've provided you.

It's all about compassion (or lack thereof). Much as we'd like to think otherwise, nobody feels compassion for everyone. There'll always be someone you'd love to see get splashed by a cab. There'll always be a table of loud, drunken people at a restaurant whom you'd like to see come down with food poisoning. There'll always be a famous movie star you'd like to see check into rehab.

You think we're horrible people now, don't you? Well, relax. We're not. Schadenfreude is a flaw, yes, but, alas, it's part of human nature—and to try to be perfect leads to far worse problems than accepting the universal flaws of the human race.

Now that you've been introduced to Schadenfreude, you'll start seeing the word everywhere. (And you'll have that strange feeling of wondering if everyone is just now starting to use it or whether it's been around forever and you've just never noticed it. It's the latter.)

Great thanks to Gary Coleman for helping us learn that it's okay to be laughed at for our own misfortunes, just as it's okay to laugh at the misfortunes of others.

And whether or not you choose to participate by laughing at the bad luck of others, be advised that people are laughing at you.

III

THE GENUINE
ARTICLE

Keeping Your Word

by Patricia Beard

It's a long way from a white lie to a whopper. But whenever a promise is broken, the distance tends to narrow.

I subscribe to a women's lecture series in New York where I am apt to run into people I don't normally see otherwise—"friendly acquaintances." Sometimes it's so nice to see them that I might get carried away and make a promise I don't intend to keep. Just a couple of months ago, after one of the lectures, I was talking with a woman I've known for a while. We like each other, but catching up in the cloakroom from time to time is probably about the right level of friendship for us. Yet, as we were putting on our coats, she said, "We should get together for lunch sometime."

"I'd like that," I said.

"Well, great," she said. "I'll call you."

"Or I'll call you," I said.

She never called me, and I didn't call her either. At first it seemed that our conversation and its aftermath made barely a scratch on the skin of my integrity or hers. Just another version of the time-honored "little white lie" I'd have said. But then I gave the matter some more thought.

These are white lies: You see a woman who's just finished a course of chemotherapy; you tell her she looks great. This is likely to do her more good than if you'd said, "You still look pretty weak; you must feel terrible." You're invited to a dinner party; you reply, "I'd love to come, but I already have plans." That's probably a better response than, "The last time we had dinner at your house, there wasn't enough food to feed a bird, and the conversation would have bored a monkey."

Is "Let's have lunch; I'll call you" any different? I think it is. Consider this: Instead of trying to avoid hurting someone's feelings, you've gone a step further by making a promise, raising expectations you won't fulfill. (Worse, you've dropped a coin into the bank that's quickly filling with cynicism, because we have begun not to count on each other's follow-through.)

White lies are remarks made to save someone's feelings. But small broken promises are acts we actually *volunteer* to perform, acts inconsequential enough that we won't be asked to account for the lapse when we break our word.

You go to an art opening and tell a young artist you're going to buy one of his paintings—you're "just boosting his confidence," but he may be counting on a sale. You promise to lend a friend a book—and forget to send it. (Or you borrow a book and don't bother to return it.) Someone admires your sweater, and you promise to fax her the phone number of the woman in Maine who knits them. You don't get around to doing it. "I'm taking my children to the circus," you say. "Why don't I take yours, too? I'll call you in the morning to check dates." You don't call. If these were broken laws, you wouldn't get more than a traffic ticket for them, but, as you may have noticed, when even parking tickets accumulate, they begin to form a picture of a certain irresponsibility.

In the same family as these lapses are the kind-sounding offers made in such a way that they're unlikely to be taken up ("Let me know what I can do when Harry gets home from the hospital"). Often, weekends in the country are vaguely proposed ("We want you to come out anytime this summer"). Even "firm" engagements are often made to be broken, so you just shrug when you're about to leave the house and your date calls to say that "something has come up." Perhaps it was inevitable that in the age of virtual realities, the next step would be virtual promises.

It wasn't always thus. Traditionally, Americans have been proud to say we are as good as our word. We used to be offended by people who didn't do what they said they would. We even labeled them with titles and expressions that indicated agreed-upon social disapproval. The man who took you out to dinner, said "I'll call you tomorrow" and never was heard from again was a "cad"; now we say he's "afraid of commitment." The committee member who promised to raise money for the hospital and didn't was "all talk and no action"; today, we might excuse her behavior because she's "overcommitted." When a successful friend of your parents offered to advise you on your career but could never find a time to meet with you, his brand of "big talk" might have reflected on his business practices. And now? We're hardly surprised when "such a busy man" can't manage to make good on a social favor.

This is not limited to personal interactions. After all, who really expects the repairman to show up between nine and twelve?

Considering all this, it begins to seem less surprising that politicians often fail to keep their promises, although they make them in public. Even the most honorable and trustworthy politicians, those who do keep their word, hire the real experts at drawing pictures in the sand—spin doctors. And who would believe *them*? It's a pretty sorry situation when those we elect to represent us seem no more bound to their word than the no-show repairman.

When you think of "Let's have lunch" as a minor subset of "If elected, I will . . ." or "Your car will be fixed by Friday so you can drive to the country," the half-promise begins to look worse. It's less like a white lie and more like a drop of acid that eats a hole in the paper on which our social contracts are written.

How do we justify it to ourselves (and others) when we squirm out of commitments made as if in good faith? We could pass the buck and blame the pace of modern life: we're all so busy we just don't have time to do every little thing we say we will. We could say that society has become so big and impersonal that private reputations don't matter much anymore. We could say the laissez-faire legacy of the sixties takes us off the hook of accountability. And speaking of hooks, we could blame the telephone, which enables us to get out of our promises without having to confront the person we're letting down.

It seems a bit limp to say it's the fault of the culture when we fail to keep our word.

Well, sure, we could blame all these ingredients of the times, and we'd be partly right. But it seems a bit limp to say it's the fault of the culture when we fail to keep our word.

Is that the way it's going to be from now on? Maybe not. The media have been chastised for requiring a level of accountability that can read as nit-picking, examining every speck of lint on the lapels of everyone from businesspeople to political leaders, in search of provenance and meaning. Sometimes this isn't much better than gossip, but perhaps such relentless scrutiny will make it harder to get away with misleading behavior in the public realm, and that will affect our private actions as well.

It seems more practical, though, not to wait for the press to shore up our social behavior but to just do it ourselves. For my part, the next time someone says "I'll call you," I am determined to have the fortitude not to hit the ball back over the net if I don't want to go on with the game. Instead I will say "It was nice to see you." Okay, it isn't much—and it won't affect the reliability of the phone installer—but it's a start. And if at first it feels awkward to be so restrained, I can always dip back into an earlier time and remind myself of what that old plain speaker, the "Yukon poet" Robert William Service, once wrote: "A promise made is a debt unpaid."

Insincerely Yours

by John Sedgwick

Tired of being thanked "for your patience" and told to
"have a nice day?" Perhaps it's time for a refresher
on speaking from the heart.

W hen my Internet service went down the other day, I knew the drill. Call customer service; be put on endless hold while a recorded voice repeatedly apologizes "for any inconvenience"; grind teeth. That's the cost of living in the modern world, I figured. For me, the profound distress came later, when a human being finally did come on the line and offered generic apologies in the same robotic tones of automated sorrow that I'd gotten from the machine.

It was the impersonality of the exchange that was so galling. The woman on the phone wasn't apologizing to me. She was merely apologizing. Indeed, she kept shifting to the first-person plural, that grand, anonymous "we," instead of the more authentic "I." And her words were pure cardboard. She didn't say anything human like "I know that can be a pain" or "It happened again? I'm so sorry!" No, she stayed relentlessly on message, like some mindless pol in front of a TelePrompTer.

It's not just my Internet service that specializes in canned speech. Key words and phrases have grown invisible quote marks around them that render them inoperative. People aren't sorry; they are "sorry," which is to say they are not sorry at all. "Have a nice day" now means something closer to "Go jump in a lake." "Thank you for your patience" is particularly empty, since, at the point we hear it, our patience is already gone.

Then again, many of these phrases are meaningless to start with. Take that "any inconvenience." The "any" is so all-inclusive, the "inconvenience" so trivializing, that the saying does nothing except dismiss my individual, unique suffering.

This phenomenon must be contagious, because so many of our everyday utterances have all the flavor, bite and food content of tofu. We don't have surgery; we undergo a "procedure." No jams for us; we experience a "situation." We don't have complaints, but "issues." Sins are out; wicked behavior is merely "inappropriate." Only postal workers are ever ticked off, venomous, ready to kill; everyone else has "concerns." Mild concerns, really, as there is no other type.

Emotionally, we seem to live in a wee world, where experiences come in one size only—small. It's like on airplanes: when pilots casually note "a little bumpiness," it really means that your 747 is being slammed by hurricane-force winds that have dropped it 1,000 feet. We have all endured the "slight delay" that leaves us baking on the tarmac for hours or been treated to the "bit of a snack," which is actually just that.

But this miniaturization comes in a more insidious form, too, one in which tiny emotions are wildly exaggerated to look like big ones. It's not just the movie critics burbling about how they "love!" some big-budget spectacular flopperoo. They find it "amazing," "incredible" or (if they're Brits) "absolutely brilliant." Everybody "loves!" everything nowadays. Which is to say they experienced mild relief that the subject in question was not quite as dull as they'd feared. Unless, of course, they "hated!" it, in which case, sadly, it was.

The plain truth, honestly expressed, is powerful stuff, and I'm not suggesting we can take too much of it. Terminal cancer, religion, an accurate description of what one person genuinely feels for another—all of these topics require delicate handling, no question. There is nothing worse in a social situation than calling a spade a spade. Or, I might add, more memorable. One time when Winston Churchill had had a few too many, an elderly constituent upbraided him: "Why, Mr. Prime Minister, you're drunk!" "Yes, madam," came the unforgettable retort, "and you are ugly. But I will be sober in the morning." To politicians nowadays, no one is ugly, least of all a voter. That same unctuous caution has caught all of us in its goo. It's not just political correctness either. Technobabble, illiteracy, bureaucratese and the fear of lawsuits have all done their bit to take the zing out of public discourse.

> People aren't sorry; they are "sorry," which is to say they are not sorry at all.

Ironically, while language in the real world is being emptied, the dramatic arts, at their best, offer us glowing examples of concise, pungent and, at times, heart-wrenching speech.

There is no question of Rick Blaine's state of mind in *Casablanca* when Humphrey Bogart utters the desperate line "Of all the gin joints in all the towns in all the world, she walks into mine." Who doesn't feel for Marlon Brando's character in *On the Waterfront* when he laments that he "could've been a contender . . . instead of a bum, which is what I am." And who among us would doubt Jack Nicholson's sincerity when, playing a crabby obsessive-compulsive writer in *As Good As It Gets,* he tells Helen Hunt, "You make me want to be a better man." Such lines may be artful, but they nonetheless convey powerful emotion directly and urgently. They connect.

But the best lines, of course, aren't lines at all. They come from the heart and go to the heart. This means skipping the bureaucratic clichés and technospeak, addressing yourself directly to your audience, telling the truth and doing your best to sound sincere. That wouldn't have brought my Internet service back, but it would have provided a connection that would have, right then, been more important—the human one between her and me.

Presume Nothing

by Jim Brosseau

Think you've got a new acquaintance all figured out?
Not so fast.

S hortly after I began working in journalism—let's just say it was a time before "impact" was widely used as a verb—I was given a graphic lesson in the perils of making assumptions. Although I can't remember what my offense was, I know that I began my explanation for it with a self-assured "I assumed. . . ."

"You assumed," my editor said mockingly. "You *assumed*?"

And then, as I watched my budding career flash before me, my boss proceeded to write something in block letters. It was the word "assume," broken into three parts. He recited an old adage I hadn't heard before. "When you assume," he said, holding up the paper on which he'd written and pointing as he went along, "you make an 'ass' out of 'u' and 'me.' "

Though the message lacked the charm of an Aesop fable, it obviously had an impact on me. In the years since, I have often, though not nearly often enough, stopped to think before acting on an assumption. I've usually been glad that I have.

Of course, we all walk around with dozens of handy assumptions swirling inside our minds: if you live in a particular community, you must be a Republican; if you're French, you're a gourmand; and, these days, if you're gay, you believe in same-sex marriage. Even in what some might think of as censor-happy times, there's still no crime against what goes on in our heads. But when we act on our assumptions—close kin to prejudices as they so often are—the social consequences can be unpleasant, and sometimes just plain sad.

The latter comes to mind when I think of my newspaper days in Philadelphia. It was a heady time, in part because I lived on stately Rittenhouse Square. Mine was not a rambling apartment in one of the area's handsome prewar buildings but a studio in one of the square's postwar high-rises. (As it was, I could barely afford it on my copy editor's salary.) Still, I had the prestigious address, and its cachet led a few people to form erroneous assumptions about my background. There was one woman in particular whose distance after an initial and quite convivial chat was a mystery to me. Then one day we bumped into each other on the street, and, speaking with the openness of two people about to leave town for other jobs, we lamented that we'd never pursued a friendship. "You lived on Rittenhouse Square," she said. "I just assumed you ran in different circles." (Well, she was partly right: I've always run in circles.)

If some things are lost because of our assumptions, other things can be gained when we put them aside. At that same Philadelphia newspaper, a summer intern I'll call Melinda was written off by a number of staffers after turning in a less-than-captivating story. I remember one editor scoffing, "Well, she's inner-city, you know," the assumption being that her prospects were decidedly limited. But I saw something promising in Melinda's writing. So, on lunch hours and over coffee breaks, I sat with this shy young woman in the newspaper's cafeteria and went over her work with her, line by line. The summer ended, and Melinda disappeared.

Fast-forward a decade to a press conference in New York City. As it broke up, there was a tap on my shoulder. I turned around to see something of a miracle: it was Melinda, smiling broadly, poised, the hand that once nearly covered her mouth whenever she spoke resting confidently at her side. She had become a magazine editor, and she'd sought me out to say thank you for the lunchroom tutorials that summer. Though I could hardly take credit for Melinda's transformation, I couldn't help wondering where her life would be had everyone along her career path stuck to the easy assumption that this "inner-city" girl couldn't shoot for the moon.

> When we act on our assumptions the social consequences can be unpleasant and sometimes just plain sad.

Thankfully, not all of our assumptions have the power to make or break careers. A lot of the things people assert based on what they assume can be so innocuous that they're best left unchallenged. If a neighbor entering the elevator takes my greeting her as a sign of affection for her mastodon on a leash, well, so be it (as long as Killer—or whatever his name is—keeps to his side of the car, of course).

Indeed, many, perhaps most, of the things we say that reflect our assumptions can be rather harmless. Which means recovering from them shouldn't be a big deal. The best approach may be the direct one, explaining why you assumed something. "You're such an Anglophile, so I thought you'd be a tea drinker." "You liked the movie so much, I figured you'd enjoy the sound track." "Your father was an avid collector of rare books, so I just assumed you'd be, too." A straightforward acknowledgment can actually be disarming. And when you're the one about whom something has been incorrectly assumed, the social compact calls for you to be gracious as well. A nice "Don't give it a second thought" can go a long way to ease a bit of embarrassment. Speaking of embarrassment, if you find it necessary to correct somebody's assumption (when, say, someone presumes you're single because you're not wearing a wedding band), do so with as little fuss as possible.

Things get trickier, though, when an assumption offends. I can't tell you how often during the Iraqi prisoner scandal I heard "white trash" (a term used blithely despite its racist undercurrents) uttered by well-educated friends and acquaintances. (But then, what was *I* assuming about the level of fairness and intelligence produced by time spent in halls of higher learning?) All the chatter breezily suggested the soldiers' misbehavior was linked to the tough economic conditions in which they were raised. But then came word that the man who did the honorable thing by reporting the abuses came from similarly humble circumstances. What a powerful illustration of how off course we can be when we make assumptions about a person's character based on his wallet or education.

These days, it seems, the socially astute find themselves putting aside a lot of assumptions in response to the world's accelerated rate of change. So they don't assume that just because a friend has a keen sense of humor, she wants her e-mail flooded with jokes. Or they think about their guests' likes and dislikes, not to mention food allergies, when hosting dinner parties or other gatherings. (There are exceptions: the chef for a Fifth Avenue family recalls how casual a few hosts could be about the snacks they served during their children's playdates.)

One meal that never goes down well is foot in mouth, and that's where a wrong-headed assumption can derail an otherwise pleasant conversation. So when you meet someone for the first time—or even an acquaintance whose political or religious leanings are unknown to you—how do you maintain an air of civility? Falling back on the lovely art of small talk is one way. The weather, family, hobbies. Chances are, the other person will drop a bead at some point, giving you a clue about where to go and not go as you converse. No beads? Why not ask a neutral question that might shake one loose, such as, "What do you think so-and-so's election chances might be?" When hot-button issues come up, try nonjudgmental words, like "interesting" or "fascinating," until your assumption is confirmed or debunked.

Clearly, not all of the missteps that result from an errant assumption ought to make us social pariahs. But if there's even the slightest possibility that our words might offend, isn't it worth the extra effort to see that they don't? After all, who wants to be thought of as a beast of burden? Certainly not "u" or "me."

Material Whirl

by Jane Hammerslough

If you get dizzy just thinking about all your possessions, perhaps it's time to stop and reassess your priorities.

I t has been estimated that the average consumer is besieged by 3,000 marketing messages a day, promising everything from a sense of belonging to inner peace, all with the quick flick of a credit card. Is it any wonder that the meaning of objects in our lives—and the expectations we have of them—has grown immensely? Possessions unquestionably hold power: a well-tailored suit makes us feel sharp; a well-built vehicle makes us feel safe. And there's certainly pleasure in giving just the right gift or purchasing something because it's beautiful. When Thorstein Veblen coined the term "conspicuous consumption" in his 1899 book, *The Theory of the Leisure Class,* he was talking about how ownership announces accomplishment. Today the stakes are even higher: acquiring objects also "guarantees" that you will satisfy your emotional and spiritual cravings. And more possessions promise even greater satisfaction.

Of course, most of us don't really think our lives, relationships and sense of well-being will be magically enhanced by yet another purchase. But even without really believing "if I own x, I'll be y," we find it tough to escape the connection, constantly articulated in magazines and on television, between buying and being. And since credit-card debt, personal bankruptcies and demand for storage space to house excess stuff are all at historic highs, it appears that some of those messages are sinking in.

So, perhaps now more than ever, in the pure pursuit of a life that takes precedence over a lifestyle, we should stop to consider what William Wordsworth wrote on the subject of materialism: "Getting and spending, we lay waste our powers."

Once we fall into the trap of possession obsession, it can be difficult to escape. No matter how many suits you own, there are always more to buy. And turning one's house into a catalog-perfect showroom may be at odds with actually enjoying time spent there. (A spilled glass of red wine could be a tragedy, after all.) The pursuit of objects ad infinitum results not just in cluttered closets but in cluttered lives. And at times it may interfere with having what we want most.

A while back I conducted a monthlong search for a couch for my den. A lovely fantasy developed: With the right couch pulling the room together, I envisioned simple, warm and cozy evenings during which nobody would argue over the remote control, tattle or scatter popcorn kernels. As the fantasy grew, my basic decision about which couch to buy blossomed into a yearning for new armchairs, a bigger television, fresh window treatments and artwork, all contributing to my picture of the harmonious family fun that would result from—and increase with—each purchase. Reality struck when one of my sons pointed out, rightly, that I was spending more weekends shopping for the family room than actually being with my family.

In fact, a time-use study by the U.S. Department of Labor

found that each week Americans spend more than three times as many hours shopping as they do playing with their children. Since an overwhelming number of us rank family as a top priority, the price, in time and energy, of "shop till you drop" may be too high.

That less might mean more was, almost literally, driven home for me when a routine roof repair unexpectedly turned into a full-blown emergency. Forced to evacuate during the resulting repairs and subsequent renovation, my family and I spent a frantic weekend packing up our possessions and moving with a few suitcases into a small, sparsely furnished rental house. During the six months we lived there, I noticed something interesting: we didn't miss much of what we'd left. We had some great times in the hideous family room; thoroughly enjoyed Christmas with a tiny tree and improvised ornaments; ate meals off mismatched plates; and survived just fine with a single laptop. In that temporary home, with its minimal storage space, we stopped accumulating so much. It felt, well, liberating.

Freed from the distraction of too many possessions, we could focus on having what we really desired.

And when we returned to our own house and began unpacking the boxes of stuff we'd hastily thrown together, I was overwhelmed by the utter excess of the stuff we'd left behind. Did we really need two pasta makers (neither of which we'd ever used), a ridiculous number of candlesticks and enough books to stock a small public library? Would we ever do anything with the platters, vases and dishes too ugly to use but too "good" to get rid of, or wear the massive quantity of shoes and clothing that we hadn't missed in half a year and hadn't worn in at least that long beforehand?

It became a reckoning of sorts, an exercise in examining our expectations of objects. And it meant questioning the fantasy future they promised and focusing on the present. As I scrutinized each object, I debated its power in our lives and became skeptical. Did we need it? Did we really want it? And did it give us pleasure or did it just sit there, demanding attention, maintenance and space?

Once we got rid of the excess, I started to see things I hadn't noticed in years. Without the clutter on the walls, I could really enjoy looking at the old map we'd hung on a once-bare spot years earlier. When we removed the extraneous kitchen items, we could actually find the things we needed while cooking. When I gave up on the fantasy family room—throwing away the huge collection of fabric swatches and buying a nice couch in an hour—I concluded that what we already owned worked pretty well. Although questioning the need for acquisitions didn't solve every problem (the kids still drop popcorn), I realized it could help make life simpler. Freed from the distraction of too many possessions, we could focus on having what we really desired— and that's something money can't buy.

Not long ago I met a woman at a party. In just five minutes I heard about her 10,000-square-foot house, her four luxury vehicles and the makes and models of her upscale kitchen appliances. I heard about the labels in her wardrobe and how, when the help didn't show up to do the laundry, she simply bought her kids new clothes. After ten minutes I knew precisely what the woman owned and planned to buy—and precisely nothing about the woman herself. Maybe there was nothing else to know. Stifling a yawn, I realized that announcing accomplishment through objects doesn't contribute much to having fun or connecting to other people in any meaningful way. When "enough" is always just a little more than you already have, you don't have a lot of room left for the truly great pleasures of life: family, friends and the time to enjoy them.

DOMESTIC
TRANQUILLITY

IV

MARRIAGE
MATTERS

The Subject Is Money

by Eileen Livers

How to prevent the topic of finances from dampening
what should be the happiest day of your life.

I n the original *Father of the Bride*, a well-meaning father
(played by Spencer Tracy) sweats over the skyrocketing
cost of his daughter's dream wedding. The year was
1950, and movie audiences certainly didn't question dear
old dad's covering all the wedding costs. Age-old tradition dictated that the bride's parents pay every expense.

By the time Steve Martin starred in the 1991 remake, the
whole premise seemed a little out of touch. Expecting a father to
foot the bill for a wedding he hadn't been consulted on, or even
seen a budget for, seemed unfair and unwise. Indeed, times have
changed. While plenty of weddings are still funded by the bride's
parents or stepparents alone, an equal number are underwritten
by the couple themselves. Sometimes the couple and their
parents decide to share the financial burden. The reasons for this
shift are many, but primary among them is that couples see
paying their own way as a means of avoiding the control issues
that often accompany accepting generous funding. Also, as brides
and grooms marry later in life, they are more financially independent and feel that covering all or a substantial part of the
wedding costs themselves is the right thing to do.

Thus, there are no longer hard and fast rules when it comes to wedding finances. How do you decide which path to follow? As a wedding expert at the women's website iVillage.com and the author of *The Unofficial Guide to Planning Your Wedding,* I've helped hundreds of brides who have grappled with that very question. The answer? Through communication and planning.

Having the Talk

Naturally, you must take some time to revel in the bliss of your engagement before you start discussing money. But it's really never too early to begin the dialogue. First and foremost, you and your betrothed must decide what kind of wedding you want. Whether you desire a gala with a twelve-piece orchestra in a grand ballroom or a more intimate affair on the beach, you'll need to mull over the elements that are most important to each of you. Be sure to consider how your ideas might affect everyone else. For example, if you're dreaming of a destination wedding, are you comfortable asking guests to cover their own travel costs? If you know your maid of honor won't be able to afford the trip, will you offer any assistance?

Think about how your parents will react to your ideas, too. If you expect them to pick up the tab for everything, will they be happy with what you have in mind? If not, would you consider funding the wedding yourselves? The more thoughtful you are ahead of time, whether you're considering your parents' wishes or your guests' wallets, the better.

When you're ready, set up a meeting with your families. Talk with one family at a time, starting with your parents. Unless you think they will be embarrassed by discussing money in front of your future spouse, meet with them together. The goal of these early conversations is to get everyone to agree on the basic wedding vision, including the budget, and to clarify who will cover the costs.

Talk with your parents about how involved they wish to be in the whole process. Since money and control almost always go hand in hand, set up your defense early on, especially if you're accepting funding from multiple sources. If you don't want everyone weighing in with opinions, be the one to come up with a plan for who will help with what. Choose items lower down on your priority list and hand out the privileges. You'll be amazed at how well received the words "This is what I would really love you to help me with" will be.

Compromising Positions

Keep in mind that these initial meetings set the mood and tone of what's to come. So while you'll want to express what matters most to you (where you plan to stand firm), you should also explain where you're willing to be flexible. That flexibility may mean increasing the size of the guest list or changing the location, as soon-to-be-wed Beth Walker did. Although the Los Angeles–based publicist originally wanted to have her wedding in Santa Barbara, California, when her father expressed his wish for it to be in the L.A. area, she relented. "It wasn't just because he was paying for the wedding," says Beth. "It was that my parents have always been there for me and for my fiancé. I wanted to have a wedding that would honor them and make everyone comfortable and happy."

Newlywed Sally Horchow's story presents a strategy worth imitating. When the television personality and freelance writer first broached the money topic with her father, he suggested that she bring him a proposed budget. That way, said Roger Horchow, his daughter could work within a set of guidelines, free to plan the Nantucket fête without constantly asking for his approval. Sally did just that, using girlfriends' wedding expenses as a bellwether. "There were items in the budget that my dad hadn't even thought about," she says. "It was good for me to list them so he'd know what to expect."

For newlywed Denise Incandela, a senior vice president at Saks Fifth Avenue, a talk with her father set forth a plan that the thirty-nine-year-old never could have imagined. "My father said he would spend up to a set sum on my wedding or give me four times that amount to purchase an apartment," she recalls. She chose door number two and happily planned every detail of the nuptials herself. "It worked out perfectly," she says.

> Today's new fiscal flexibility may at times cause confusion and even a little discomfort.

"I didn't have to battle with my parents. And I avoided having inconceivable conversations with my father, like why the flowers were costing ten thousand more than we'd budgeted. I'm too old for that."

Going It Alone

If you and your groom decide to cover the wedding costs yourselves, be aware that your parents may feel rejected. Be sure to tell them that their kindness and generosity are appreciated. And consider accepting a small sum from them. You can even consult with them about allocating the cash for something other than the wedding, such as your honeymoon or a new car.

Today's new fiscal flexibility may at times cause confusion and even a little discomfort, but this break in tradition is also beneficial. It's good to have open conversations about who will pay for what. If such talks help prevent painful budget battles and control tugs-of-war later—and they should—then you and your families can stop money from interfering with the spirit and joy of your wedding day. Just imagine: if another remake of *Father of the Bride* were to be released today, dear old dad might actually get to enjoy the wedding.

Matrimonial Manners

by Stacey Okun

How to have a memorable wedding without
forgetting the ones who can make it so.

With old wedding traditions to honor and more recent ones to consider, the etiquette maze faced by newly engaged couples has never been more daunting. Although the road to perfect nuptials has no short-cuts, the following excerpt, taken from *Town & Country Elegant Weddings* (Hearst Books), provides a good compass.

Gender Issues

Today's brides and grooms are making some unusual choices when it comes to their wedding parties: asking the people who are closest to them to be in their wedding often means calling on friends of the opposite sex. Some brides break with tradition by naming a close male friend as a "bridesmaid" or "maid of honor." You can bet these fellows are not wearing gowns in any shape or form but rather boutonnières to match the color of the female bridesmaids' dresses. Some couples do away with the bridal party altogether, asking family and close friends to participate in the ceremony instead. The bottom line is that a wedding is an occasion for closeness and warmth. Choosing the people who mean the most to you is more important than selecting those who are the right gender. As for the Goldman Sachs investment banker who walked down the aisle to the altar with his dog? These days, it seems, man's best friend can also be man's best man.

Welcome Wagon

Out-of-town weddings can be costly for the guests. To help them plan, prepare a separate card sent with, or immediately following, the wedding invitation, listing a variety of recommended hotels in every price range. Etiquette dictates that the couple and/or their families provide a welcome dinner for the out-of-town guests. The rehearsal dinner, traditionally hosted by the groom's family, usually serves this purpose, but if not all out-of-town guests are invited, cocktails and dinner should be offered at a separate location. When guests are staying at the same hotel where an evening wedding is to take place, a hospitality suite offering coffee, juices and simple sandwiches during the day should also be available, if possible. Holding a brunch or a lunch for guests at a nearby home is an appropriate alternative.

Lending Institution

"Something old, something new, something borrowed, something blue." Adhering to this maxim is an age-old custom, one that has surprisingly endured, even among today's brides. The challenge? Finding something borrowed, preferably jewelry. If someone doesn't offer to lend you a piece to wear at your wedding, how do you go about, well, borrowing one? The best approach is to write a short but sweet note to the person who has something special to lend and who also means something special to you. (The bottom line: don't request anything intimate from someone with whom you are not intimate.) The note should read something like this:

"Dear Aunt Barbara: I've always admired your diamond bracelet and would love to wear it as 'something borrowed' on my wedding day, not only because it is beautiful but also because it is yours. I will gratefully return it the evening of my wedding . . . ."

Flattered, the recipient of the note is unlikely to refuse and likely to be quite touched.

If the Music's Too Loud . . .

No matter how wonderful the band sounds, the music is still likely to be too loud for the guests whose table is closest to the bandstand. Of course, if the location allows, all the tables can be set back from the music, although most ballrooms and clubs don't have ample space for that luxury. So the question is: who should sit closest to the band? The answer: the people who are most likely to be on the dance floor for the majority of the party, which usually means the youngest guests. A table of teenagers might actually enjoy the spot closest to the band; a table of twenty-somethings probably won't mind either, if they're occupied with the dancing.

> The bottom line is that a wedding is an occasion for closeness and warmth.

Having Your Cake

At some point after the wedding cake makes its grand entrance, tradition dictates that the bride cut a piece and feed a bite to the groom and then he feed a bite to her. The act represents their first shared, sweet moment as a married couple, and it should be handled with a certain amount of decorum. In fact, today's brides eschew the longtime tradition of the groom's smashing a piece of cake into the bride's face, deeming it immature. Los Angeles wedding planner Mindy Weiss swears she can always tell how long a marriage is going to last by the way the groom feeds the cake to his bride. "If he's gentle and doesn't let the cake get on the bride's dress, they're going to be OK," she says. "If he smashes it in her face: divorce." The moment should always be in good taste, but it can have some humor. "One groom put icing on the bride's nose and licked it off," recalls Weiss, "and I got the feeling that they were going to have a very happy, funny life together."

Flower Power

What happens to the flower arrangements when the wedding is over? Guests should never take arrangements home unless they are specifically invited to do so. Often the hosts save the wedding flowers for a postwedding brunch and then discard them. Once all the festivities are over, the flowers should be donated to a needy recipient. Contact a local hospital or nursing home to arrange for delivery the day after the wedding. Then request that your florist donate the time to transport them by van. There is no reason that your wedding flowers shouldn't have a long, happy life, too.

Stepping Down the Aisle

by Martha Woodham

Here come the mother and father of the bride
and (often) their new spouses.

ivorce is a word rarely found in my vintage
etiquette books. More pages are given over
to how to eat a lobster in polite company
than how to handle divorce or stepparents.

Proper ladies and gentlemen didn't
divorce; they coexisted, and the etiquette
writers never dealt with the problem of where to seat the father
of the bride's new wife at a wedding, because she was expected to
stay home.

My copy of Emily Post's 1930 *Etiquette* devotes just two
pages to "When the Parents of the Bride Are Divorced." In her
primary scenario, Post describes Mary, a bride who has been
lovingly reared by her mother. Mary's father—the cad!—"has
shown no concern" for his daughter. Mary's mother, who remarried after her divorce, is advised to send wedding invitations
"exactly as though Mary's real father were actually as well as
legally dead."

As for the divorced parents of a groom, Post dismisses their
estrangement as "not noticeable." The mother of the groom
stands in the receiving line at the reception, of course, and "her

former husband and his second wife may with propriety be guests at the reception, but they naturally avoid approaching his former wife." The possibility that the father of the groom may be on his third or fourth marriage is not even considered.

Sad to say, seventy-five years later, the tide of divorce has become a flood, and more than 40 percent of today's marriages are put asunder. Many of them are so-called starter marriages, childless unions that last only a year or two. But chances are that if there's a wedding, there's probably a divorce somewhere on one side of the aisle or the other. Often it's a messy one, and there may be multiple stepparents.

The stories are not pretty. As an author of two books on wedding etiquette and an adviser to brides on matters of taste for the past fourteen years, I've been privy to nuptials that range from the sublime to the sublimely tacky. And some stories are so heartrending, I often feel like the Ann Landers of weddings. Most questions from brides (rarely grooms!) deal with divorce. One bride so despaired over getting her feuding parents to act amicably that she ended up having two receptions, one for each parent and his or her spouse.

> Weddings have traditions that are etiquette minefields for brides and grooms with multiple stepparents.

One would think that parents could put aside their animosities for the few hours that it takes to get their offspring married, but weddings have traditions that are etiquette minefields for brides and grooms with multiple stepparents. A tradition as simple as who sits where can balloon into a festering mass of hurt feelings and angry words quicker than a minister can say "Dearly beloved."

Here is a sampling of the etiquette questions I often receive from brides:

What responsibilities does the stepmother have in the wedding-planning process, particularly if her husband, the bride's father, is paying for the wedding?

Unless she raised the bride, a stepmother should not expect to have any control over the wedding. She can, however, offer her assistance in running errands and handling mundane tasks for the bride and her mother. Money issues can lead to resentment from first wives, who usually think their children are owed elaborate weddings, and subsequent wives, who may struggle financially to subsidize them. To avoid misunderstandings, the couple should agree to a budget with the father of the bride and stick to it.

What if the stepmother is younger than the bride?

She should act older than her years and never, ever try to upstage the bride. If she was a factor in the breakup of the bride's parents' marriage and there is lingering bitterness, she should offer to do the right thing and stay home on the wedding day.

What is the role of a biological parent if he or she has not been a continuing presence in the bride's or groom's life?

Absent parents should not show up just before a wedding and expect to be greeted with open arms. The stepparent who has been a real father or mother to the bride or groom should be given the traditional parental honors of escorting the bride down the aisle and sitting in the front pew.

What is appropriate wedding-day attire for the mothers and stepmothers?

Just as the mother of the groom takes her fashion cue from the attire of the bride's mother, so should stepmothers.

What if a bride has more than one stepparent? And what if she feels closer to stepfather Number Two than stepfather Number One or even her own father?

The bride has several options: she can be escorted down the aisle by a brother or another male family member; she can walk with her mother; or she can walk alone. Some brides opt to have one father escort them part of the way down the aisle before switching off to another—just like a baton in a relay race.

Who gives the bride away if she has a close relationship with all of her "fathers"?

It is an honor usually given to her biological father, but only the bride can decide the answer. When the presider asks the congregation "Who gives this woman to be married?" the one who has escorted her to the altar can be inclusive and say, "Her family and I do."

Who sits where at the ceremony?

The front pews are reserved for the mothers of the bride and groom and their husbands, with the bride's family on the left and the groom's on the right. If the relationship is friendly, stepmothers are seated along with the fathers in the second or third row. If not, they are seated farther back. By the way, unless the bride and groom request special treatment for them, stepmothers are escorted into the service by an usher and seated just like any other wedding guest.

Receptions bring another set of problems, but limited space prevents me from exploring them here. However, "The Gracious Stepparent's Ten Commandments," from my book *Wedding Etiquette for Divorced Families,* offers a quick guide. Here are some of my favorites:

- Do not insist that your name be on the invitations, even if etiquette dictates that it should be.
- Do not fret when your spouse is asked to pose for family photos that include his or her ex.
- Do not insist on standing in the receiving line.
- Do not implore that your children be part of the wedding party.
- Do throw a party for the couple, but don't upstage the festivities hosted by the father or mother.
- Do not try to outdo the parents in any way by dressing or acting in a manner that draws attention to yourself. Remember: this is not your day.

But perhaps the best commandment is the simplest: life's short; play sweet.

V
EVER AFTER

To Love and to Cherish?

by Janet Carlson Freed

Think twice before you roll your eyes at your spouse;
such disrespectful gestures speak volumes
about your marriage.

Years ago, a wise if disillusioned friend of mine mused, "If only we'd treat the people we love like we treat the people we don't love." He was referring to the tendency to hold doors for strangers and be polite to the grocery cashier but then go home and take out our bad mood or frustration on our beloved. Why do we indulge in lapses of manners among the people we care about most? Because, well, we can. We feel safe; they accept us and will stay with us through thick and thin, till death do us part—or so we assume, despite the glaring divorce statistics. Such thoughtless behavior is called shooting yourself in the foot. Maybe it's worse than that; it's shooting your marriage in the heart.

Not that I'm an expert (I've been rude to my husband occasionally, and he to me), but I think manners are best applied to those we love. Manners aren't window dressing, nor are they about conforming to social ideals; they are a matter of making the other person comfortable, happy or safe. In a conversation with my ballroom-dance coach, whose expertise is partnership,

I came to appreciate how functional manners can be. When we first started dancing together, he said, "My job is to think about your comfort as we dance, and your job is to think about my comfort. Forget about yourself; you'll feel a lot better." This makes for a successful spin around the room to the music, but it also struck me as beautifully applicable to the marriage partnership.

If love, which presumably fuels a marriage, means wanting the best for the other person, then love, logically, generates manners between spouses. Ah, if it were as simple as that, we wouldn't need marriage counselors, *Men Are from Mars, Women Are from Venus* or a fifty-fifty opportunity to exit through the divorce door. More than thirty years of studies of married couples conducted by John Gottman, professor emeritus of psychology at the University of Washington, indicate that an important predictor of divorce, surprisingly enough, is a fleeting, seemingly teensy-weensy transgression that demonstrates a major failure of attitude: eyeball rolling after a spouse's comment or gesture. Uh-oh. Just as bad is the stone-faced stare into space, which speaks loud and clear of emotional withdrawal, deadly to any marriage.

There's hope for us, says Gottman, author of *The Seven Principles for Making Marriage Work*. His research shows that it's the ratio of positive to negative expressions—critical, contemptuous, defensive or dismissive body language or verbalizations—that counts. A solid marriage has a ratio of twenty to one (five to one during an argument). If you have a slightly weaker ratio, it might be useful to look at what's behind the negative expressions.

What do bad manners mean in a marriage? Is love so short-lived? Is a touch of mean-spiritedness innate to human beings? Or does the disrespect hint of the inevitable emotional stew of unresolved anger and resentment below the surface? I spoke with Steven Goldstein, a clinical psychologist in New York City, about the little behaviors that are big betrayals.

"The context is so big—love, marriage, the fantasy or yearning that the other person will at some deep level take care of you—that the small things, like manners, can seem trivial," says Goldstein. "Actually, the small things are a reflection of the big."

Most of us go into marriage with high hopes, he continues, particularly the hope that this other person is going to make our dreams come true. "When you realize that your dream isn't going to be fulfilled, the low is so profound. And the disappointment gets played out in the small things—the little criticisms between spouses, for example—but it feels bigger." The negative behaviors are smoke signals originating from the vast disappointment that we are not going to be rescued or completed by our partner; that disappointment masquerades as anger and resentment.

Understanding the root of spousal rudeness is a start. What to do next? Exercise self-control? Goldstein advises, "The object is not just to gain control of your behavior, but to seize an opportunity to grow. Becoming aware of the part of you that is not respecting your spouse gives you the chance to integrate parts of yourself you've been ignoring and to change your relationship. It's hard work—particularly in a long marriage in which bad manners have become chronic."

Minding manners then becomes not the goal but a tool for enriching the partnership. "Having good manners," says Goldstein, "is really to hear and try to understand the other person." Or, as Buddhist monk Thich Nhat Hanh suggests, perhaps it's to wake each morning and treat your spouse like a stranger, delighting in all the sparkling aspects of this new person.

There's more hard work in practicing such mindfulness. It's a rare person who, when sorely tempted to stomp out of the room, can stop and listen with compassion. Goldstein's advice is to go slowly. "Think of helping the offender to know that you understand what he's saying." Other experts, like John Gottman, flout conventional wisdom and recommend going to bed angry: "It may be beneficial to continue the discussion with cooler heads in the morning."

I've noticed some successfully married couples are committed to the idea that you don't *find* the right person, you *be* the right person. "I think it's up to us to communicate to other people how we'd like to be treated," says Cynthia Roeth, of Tarrytown, New York. "When my husband Neil and I were dating, he was always on time and I was ten to fifteen minutes late. I commented on his punctuality, and he said, 'I think it's the right way to treat people.' I changed right then and there. I made the decision to honor him. He hadn't preached or criticized me. He'd shown good manners. Now, most often, we're together at the appointed time, waiting for other people!"

> Having good manners is really to hear and try to understand the other person.

Certainly, it's easier to honor thy true love in the early days. Roeth says the key is to keep it up. Like many long-married spouses, she and her husband know that happily-ever-after is not the prize won on the wedding day but a choice to be made, and demonstrated, every single day of married life.

A Little Respect, Please

These are ways of showing your loyalty and love—or lack thereof:

- Don't interrupt or get into a Ping-Pong match of contradicting each other.
- Don't reveal negative things about your spouse to others. Some couples treat this as a competitive sport in public, and both wind up losers.
- Don't complain at social events. Say it to your partner privately.
- Don't fidget when he's talking.
- Don't show embarrassment on behalf of your spouse when his joke falls flat or her opinion is un-P.C. Speak up in a neutral way.
- Don't think the kids don't read your signals. They pick up on body language even better than verbal statements. Consider what you're teaching them about relationships.
- Do make eye contact, even after twenty years.
- Do hold hands. It's fun.
- Do laugh at his joke if it's funny, but be sincere. No fawning.
- Do go for a little witty repartee with your spouse, but keep it compassionate. Ask yourself if you'd engage in the same verbal sparring with your boss or your best friend.
- Do tolerate your differences. You might enjoy a fresh perspective.

Penny-wise,
Meet Pound-foolish

by David Brown

When one spouse's largesse collides with the other's thrift,
compromise requires more than just a good calculator.

C an marriage work between a profligate man and a frugal—I'm resisting saying stingy—woman? I had always thought that one's attitude toward money could wreck a relationship, and it has certainly been an issue in my marriage to Helen Gurley Brown.

What first attracted me to Helen, apart from her good looks and her style, was the revelation that she had paid cash for her Mercedes-Benz 190SL. I had never before met a girl who paid cash for so much as a pack of cigarettes, never mind a car. I thought, "Here is a free-spending and solvent creature." Alas, I was mistaken. Solvent, yes, but I later learned that she had cried for days after paying out that cash. I discovered—far too late—that I was involved with a saver and a skinflint.

My wife and I are both Depression babies, born and brought up when nearly everyone was broke and more people were out of work than had jobs. Helen came from dirt-poor Arkansas, while I was from Wall Street's favorite playground, Long Island. Even after my family's home was sold to pay taxes following the crash,

I would regularly forget that I was no longer rich—and I spent accordingly. This hang-up stayed with me through the years.

When Helen and I married, she couldn't imagine why a highly paid Hollywood executive had no savings and was, in fact, in debt. (Two divorces were among my extravagances.) Thus, she had also been deceived by my spending habits. To this day she becomes furious when she recalls the $200 Christmas gift I gave the maître d' at the long-since-closed Romanoff's, a far costlier gift than the string of faux pearls I had given her.

I continue to bestow pricey presents on captains, waiters and, in one fiery incident, the busboy at Mark's, a private London club, who never forgot the £20 note he pocketed for clearing the table. After our argument at the table about the tip, Helen and I continued the discussion in the reception hall, where she, cross about my "generosity," virtually screamed as she headed out the door, stomping her way back to Claridge's all alone. For my part, I was left to contemplate never being allowed back in Mark's, considering that no major enthusiasm exists in the United Kingdom for screamers of either sex. (Truth be told, I *did* get back in. The busboy must have put in a good word.)

As for me, I never miss an opportunity to waste money.

It gets worse. Sometimes when I have left $30 on a dresser for the maid in a hotel we've stayed in only one night, Helen does a little reconnaissance after I've gone out into the hall with the luggage. Picking up one of the tens, she'll insist it is her money that I'm throwing out the window.

Of course, she can change direction in a microsecond when something doesn't cost what she thought it would. For example, Helen's improbable romance with caviar began years ago at New York's posh Le Pavillon restaurant. A captain appeared with a big blue can of beluga caviar and proceeded to ladle out giant quantities. Helen was aghast, imagining a bill approximating the United States GDP. No, she protested, until the captain said, "Mr. Brown's secretary gave Mr. Soulé [the restaurant's proprietor] a tour of the 20th Century Fox studio, and he wishes to say thank you." From that day forward, Helen's taste for caviar escalated, augmented by free, gigantic portions on the *QE2*, where she often had lecture dates.

As for me, I never miss an opportunity to waste money. At a dinner honoring me at New York's Dutch Treat Club, my friend Gene Shalit observed that the occasion was an anomaly inasmuch as I always pick up the check and never "go Dutch." Okay, maybe I'm a little over the top with dispensing money. Given the choice, I used to take the Concorde to London or Paris, although I'd accumulated a million American Airlines frequent-flier miles on my credit card.

The upside of having a parsimonious wife is that it has turned me from being an economic illiterate into someone who knows and cherishes the value of money. After we opened a savings account, I enjoyed seeing our balance go up each week. And when Helen offered to make out checks for nothing, I said good-bye to my business manager, who received 5 percent of my income for paying bills. (The fact that she was blonde and foxy hastened her departure.)

Helen's ways have not changed. When the kitchen of our

Pacific Palisades home needed redoing, she hired a handy local fireman rather than a costly kitchen specialist. She never discards paper clips. If I place the day's change on our hall table, she appropriates it for bus fare—at the senior rate, of course. Flight attendants, knowing her hoarding habits, give her mini gin and Scotch bottles.

So far as I can remember, Helen has never bought any office supplies for home use. (Some of the pencils, erasers and memo pads that we have at home date back to her secretarial years at the Foote, Cone & Belding advertising agency.) Our biggest arguments are over whether to take a taxi or a bus. The bus wins. She'd take a bus in a blizzard on New Year's Eve.

There you have it: a penny-pinching—to put it mildly—wife and a spendthrift husband. The money she saves, I squander. So how do we manage money and marriage? My rules for preventing this issue from erupting into relationship-busting flare-ups are:

- If your mate or life partner is on an asset-wasting spending spree, he (or she) must be stopped. Credit cards must be destroyed, charge accounts closed, bank accounts frozen. Terminal profligacy must be treated as an addiction. Intervention must be arranged, with family members and financial advisers in attendance.

- Big-time compulsive gambling is incurable. A divorce lawyer is the only possible therapist. Act swiftly before your house is gone.

- This is for wives: Is your husband secretive about his financial status? A change in his spending may signal munificence toward another woman.

- Are you being dunned by creditors when you have no recollection of spending money or incurring debt? You may be the victim of a spouse's prodigal habits.

- Remember: You are liable to the IRS if your mate doesn't pay taxes.

Despite the acrimonious difference between our spending habits, Helen and I pool our funds. Our bank accounts, stock portfolio and real estate are held jointly, with either of us able to clean out the other with one signature and no recourse.

Obviously, this arrangement succeeds because of our total trust. How else could Helen put up with my ordering a $150 bottle of Château Lafite Rothschild at New York's '21' Club when I was freshly unemployed? Richer or poorer, we are the spend/thrift couple. For us, it works.

VI
MOTHERHOOD

So, What Do You Expect?

by Jill Kargman

Baby on the way? Look to be pampered,
but don't become an *enfant terrible*.

S ince becoming pregnant, I have been astounded by the number of moms-to-be who turn into divas. It's one thing to accept a seat on a crowded bus, but it's another matter entirely to demand treatment befitting Cleopatra. An example: While I waited in line recently at a neighborhood movie theater, a woman pranced to the front and announced, "I'm pregnant!" It was as if pregnancy gave her government clearance to cut in. "So am I," I said fruitlessly from the back of the line.

I can't fathom why some pregnant women feel that they suddenly deserve VIP status. On the one hand, it's common courtesy for them to be shown to a table in a restaurant before the rest of their party has arrived. But why do they act as if everything should be served to them on a silver platter?

When my mother was nine months pregnant with yours truly, she patiently stood in line for an hour—in the pouring rain—to purchase tickets for a Bette Midler concert. Not once did it occur to her that she needn't wait her turn along with everyone else. After all, she was pregnant, not sick.

While I've certainly been exposed to divahood on all levels, it was not until I became pregnant myself that I began to encounter so many type-A moms-to-be. Many of these high-powered ladies attended the nation's top universities and quickly ascended the ranks in their careers as bankers, lawyers and corporate VPs. After they got pregnant, their ambition and boardroom drive got funneled into the fetus. And these mothers approach their new roles with the same foaming-at-the-mouth ferocity and yearning for success as they did their old ones. Witness those moms who look at nursery schools while their baby is still in utero.

I started to get scared of these aggressive, achievement-oriented moms after I announced my pregnancy. These "helpful" sorts have succeeded only in making me feel overwhelmed. They have given me more than twenty-five books and faxed thirty-page spreadsheets of "necessary" baby buys. (Many of these women registered for their baby-shower gifts at seven shops.) I have also been attacked by swarms of "experts" who have given me hot tips like the names of $2,000 "babyproofers" (who do such things as putting plastic safety locks on their clients' toilets) and top clothiers (at kiddie-couture prices). Haven't these people ever heard of Old Navy?

If only the fashion frenzy were just for the little one on the way. The chic maternity stores that seem to have cropped up everywhere often sell exorbitantly priced items, even though they'll be used for only a few months. Worse still, one prominent expectant mother was recently quoted as saying "I don't do that maternity thing; I just go into Michael Kors or Marc Jacobs, buy something oversized and have it altered to fit around my belly." Then there are the women in their ninth month who teeter around on Jimmy Choo or Manolo Blahnik stilettos, no matter that their stomachs are in a different zip code. Girls, what are you doing? Put your feet up! Crack open some Ben & Jerry's! It's as if these women can't look bad for a single moment of their pregnancy. God forbid they had to endure an evening when their usual high style was sacrificed for comfort.

But no. A type-A diva's appearance—pregnant or nay—is key. And some women have such ambitious social agendas that they wouldn't miss the opening of an envelope, heedless of the swollen midriff protruding from under their cashmere sweaters.

The main thing these moms-to-be must understand is that after years of aiming for perfection at work, at home and even in their weddings (obviously, many Bridezillas someday become Momzillas), when they're expecting a baby, they can't always be in control. They must relinquish all desperate attempts to have everything in order, Filofax style, if only because there is obvious chaos built into pregnancy: all sorts of symptoms, body changes, and the uncertainty of what lies ahead. When you are pregnant, there is a mysterious creature growing inside you, and you can't possibly know how it will feel to give birth or to see the face of your child for the first time. It is the ultimate test of patience. But some women, it seems, can't handle the nine months that nature intended.

Indeed, I've noticed a rash of early, planned C-sections, arranged so that moms don't have to deal with those pesky nine months of weight gain and waiting. It started with celebrities who pushed their obstetricians to perform Cesareans at eight-and-a-half months. Now other women are catching on. One of my friends even advised me to schedule a Cesarean ASAP, saying, with a knowing look, "*Trust me.* Your husband will thank you for it." When I inquired if radical abdominal surgery was really the way to go, choruses of elective C-section vets swore by it, saying that they felt nothing during the delivery and that they were spared the last torturous weeks of pregnancy.

I happen to believe that those weeks are part of the process for a reason. So I'm going to leave my baby's birthday to nature. Not that I'm eager for the pain—bring on the epidural!—but there will be no scalpels used weeks before my due date to avoid excess bloating. Control is something many women, myself included, are used to having; it's part of who we are. But for the passage into motherhood, I feel that I have to just let go. If I tried to prepare for it the way an account exec prepares for a new business pitch, I'd be in for a serious wake-up call once I discovered that I can't hold all of the reins.

So as these type-A women exhale and get set for labor and a new being in their lives, perhaps the best thing for them to realize is that divas can love themselves and still pour their hearts and smarts into the baby who's arriving. One of the hardest things for detail-oriented people to do is expect the unexpected, but with a new baby, every second brings an element of glorious surprise and the miraculous perspective of seeing things for the very first time.

> Some women have such ambitious social agendas that they wouldn't miss the opening of an envelope, heedless of the swollen midriff protruding from under their cashmere sweaters.

Going Public
by Stacey Okun

Need to answer your hungry child's call? Here are a few tips
to quiet both your baby and the strangers around you.

T hey're everywhere, it seems. In restaurants, bookstores, museums and, of course, the playground. I even saw them at the movies once—before the lights were dimmed. Breasts. Not just any breasts, but ones with a maternal purpose. It's the most natural thing in the world, a mother suckling her child. Unless, that is, you're the one watching. For no matter how natural a thing it may be, it is still a most intimate act. As a thirty-something woman who breast-fed her two children—albeit never in public—I must admit that I, too, am uncomfortable being a witness to public breast-feeding.

Reactions to breast-feeding range from admiration and curiosity to disgust and full-fledged heckling. Case in point: A friend was feeding her newborn in a park when a passing bicycle messenger screamed out, "Hey lady, got milk?" Suddenly, everyone in the vicinity turned around to stare.

Of course, there was a time when all women did what came naturally without thinking twice. Breast-feeding has been a part of bringing up a healthy baby since the days of Adam and Eve. In fact, before the nineteenth century, when baby bottles as we know them were invented, breast-feeding was the only mode of feeding an infant. Whether it was done in public or private depended a lot on culture, socioeconomic class and the mores of the day. Recent studies on the benefits of breast-feeding have prompted greater numbers of women to opt for the natural route rather than use formula. That pleases the American Academy of Pediatrics, which recommends that all mothers breast-feed their newborns at least until their first birthday.

So, with the experts actually saying "Go forth and breast-feed," it's clear that breast-feeding has become ensconced in both our private and, yes, public lives. More than twenty states have enacted laws clarifying that women have the right to breast-feed in public; some states will even fine an establishment that asks a nursing woman to leave its premises.

Being a bit modest, I rarely roamed farther than a few blocks from my home when I was with one of my breast-fed children. If either of my sons emitted a "Feed me!" whimper, I headed for my favorite rocking chair—and fast. I must confess, however, that I chose to breast-feed my children for only three months each. Had I decided to breast-feed for a full year, remaining so close to home would have been very confining. But even for mothers who breast-feed in private, at some point during the course of their child's first year, he is likely to scream his own version of "Got milk?" at the top of his little lungs in the middle of a department store, a museum, an airport terminal or a restaurant. At times like this, the only way to sate the famished tot is, in the rather blunt words of my bemused husband, to "whip 'em out."

How do we deal with this delicate issue? Let's start with the onlookers. When faced with a breast-feeding mom, first put yourself in her exhausted place. She may simply have no choice but to feed her child right then and there. If you cannot escape the situation, your best bet is to look the other way and try to forget about it. As for the mothers themselves, there are many ways to take observers' sensitivities into account when breast-feeding:

- When going out with the baby, be sure to plan ahead. Wear something that will cover most of your breast when nursing. If your baby will take an occasional bottle, try to schedule that bottle at the time of day when you'll be in public together. Another option is to use a breast pump. I found pumps to be horrifying devices, but they are useful. Simply pump enough milk for a feeding, fill a bottle and bring it along in an insulated bag.

- Engage in a few moments' worth of thoughtful observation and choose the best possible place to breast-feed. The ladies' lounge of a department store or restaurant is ideal, of course. So is a corner table in a restaurant, where you can face your chair toward the wall. Other options include a quiet nook in a bookstore or the last row of a movie theater (if you must). All of these locations have the advantage of being "privately public."

- When with close friends or family, take into account what you know about them and try to anticipate what their reactions might be. "The first time I breast-fed in front of my very conservative father-in-law, I saw him shudder when he heard a sucking noise coming from underneath my shirt," says one California woman who prides herself on being considerate. "I decided it just wasn't worth making him feel uncomfortable, so when he was around, I'd move to another room when my baby got hungry."

- Be gracious to people who seem to be having a problem with your public nursing. If you see them squirming, try to face the other way. If they approach you with a complaint, you might respond "I'm sorry you feel that way. I'll try to be more discreet." Being a mother, after all, means you're in for a lifetime of pacifying people.

- Most important, under no circumstances should you compromise your child's well-being because you're embarrassed or afraid someone will comment. If your beautiful baby is starting to cry for food, listen to those folks at Nike; just do it. If polled, most onlookers, I think, would prefer a quietly suckling baby to a screaming one.

> When faced with a breast-feeding mom, first put yourself in her exhausted place.

When all else fails, it doesn't hurt to have a sense of humor about public breast-feeding. My three-year-old son recently watched a woman feeding her baby at a frozen-yogurt shop we frequent. We happened to catch her just as she was switching the baby from one breast to the other. "What's that baby doing, Mommy?" he asked. "Eating," I replied. When he got to the counter, he informed the yogurt man, "I want two scoops, too." Children, it seems, can be the most gracious observers of all.

How to Treat Your Nanny

by Janet Carlson Freed

You may be her boss, but she's not just any employee.
It's a tricky relationship, built on much more than
a thank-you and a paycheck.

My two-year-old daughter, Erica, called me "Ku-mommy" one Saturday morning, and I took it as a signal that I had succeeded in forging a nearly perfect relationship with our nanny. Her name is Kumarie (Koo-MAR-ee), and she is from Trinidad. If Erica, who was two months old when she met Kumarie, can confuse us, then I can go to my office every day without quite so much working-parent guilt. It's possible my child doesn't feel "left" with a sitter; instead she feels she has two mothers. Or, more precisely, the two of us caregivers merge in her naive psyche as one complete mother figure, poetically named Ku-mommy.

Some mothers are jealous when their children call the baby-sitter "Mommy." I can understand that, but I myself don't experience jealousy. For many of us, raising a child today requires dropping the barriers of the nuclear family. Our modern definition of the extended family may not include far-flung aunts and uncles, but it does embrace the nanny and the next-door neighbors.

I'll never forget the first morning I walked out the door and left my nine-month-old firstborn daughter, Alden, in the hands of a stranger, hoping for the best. Was I crazy? No crazier, I suppose, than the rest of this country full of dual-income families. For the most part, the caregiver arrangement works out fine, but there's no ignoring the fact that we're taking a gamble. I'm not alone in recalling with a shudder the trial of British nanny Louise Woodward, whom the prosecutor portrayed as "frustrated, unhappy, resentful." Can any of us afford a babysitter who is those things? Who among us would not go to the farthest extreme, not just to hire the right person in the first place but then to do the far more difficult work of cultivating the best possible relationship with her? It's an unending project that calls on all the resources in our nature. Management skills are part of it, but just as important are the skills of humanity: empathy, generosity—all staples of good manners.

Thinking of the nanny, babysitter or au pair as family (since she shares in the responsibility for the welfare of the children) shows her the respect she deserves. She is, after all, different from any other "household employee" in that she's required to be your surrogate and look after what you prize most in the world. For her to do so necessitates that she bond with your children, indeed love them. That's asking a great deal of any employee. To me, the modern reality is that my husband and I have a partner in parenting—in our case, one who has raised three adorable daughters of her own. As a mother, Kumarie has ten years on me. This makes her more of an expert than I. (Actually, I view us as just a couple of working girls.) I respect her work. No, that's too restrained. I worship the ground she walks on, because my girls are happy, and she makes my life, such as I have arranged it, possible.

To say that things are downright collegial between Kumarie and me would be false and patronizing. I am the manager; she works for me. But the delicate balance we sustain, between one good mother and another, is buoyed by a mutual respect for the gray areas of life and the calling of motherhood.

Although we have an excellent relationship now, for a time it was a bumpy ride. Sometimes the competition between two matriarchs under the same roof got pretty heavy. What competition? Certainly there's nothing gray about Kumarie's official job description, which, as most families do, I put on paper from the outset: child care, light housekeeping (which means tidying up after the kids), driving to and from activities, and weekly grocery shopping. Seems clear enough. But as I pictured myself doing the work Kumarie does, I wondered if I wouldn't tend to do things my way, which I naturally considered the better way.

We struggled, for example, over grocery receipts. I'd give Kumarie a blank check and a list. I needed the receipt to mark the total in my checkbook and in case I had to return something. Often, there'd be no receipt on the table when I came home. It happened time and again. At first I was puzzled, then angry. Unable to sort it out, I did the shopping myself on Saturdays.

Then there was the daily diary our previous babysitters had been keeping since our daughters were born. Like any besotted mom, I loved reading it when I came home in the evening—what Alden had eaten, how many steps Erica had taken—and the sitters had all obliged. But I found I had to remind Kumarie constantly about jotting things down. I'd leave her those reminders every morning on yellow sticky notes atop the kitchen counter (our command central), to no avail.

Finally, one day, my husband and I sat down to talk with Kumarie about why the tension in the house had grown so thick. Generally, in such instances, I think, people assume the babysitter is somehow at fault, that she's moody or has an attitude; we gave ours the benefit of the doubt. She'd come to us a shy, reserved woman, and we accepted that. Nevertheless, communication was needed here. Kumarie opened up at last and told me that she didn't like coming to work each morning to a barrage of yellow notes. Okay, she had a point there. I agreed to back off. But I stood firm on the grocery receipts. And we compromised on the daily diary by creating a weekly log sheet on the computer.

Thinking of the nanny, babysitter or au pair as family shows her the respect she deserves.

That was a turning point in our relationship. We had worked out some practical solutions and learned a few lessons. Two different worlds merging in one house need to make an effort to see things from each other's point of view. I discovered I had been expecting Kumarie to act like my coworkers. I'd bring home my turbocharged negotiating style and impose it on her. And I'd mistaken my eagerness to talk with an ability to speak her language. Soon, it became easier for Kumarie to communicate with me. We became more tolerant of our differences. There is, after all, more than one way to load the dishwasher. And, I've even come to see, more than one way to raise my children. Now I try to stick to these fundamentals:

• Don't sweat the small stuff. Tackle the major issues and let the rest slide, at least until the moment is right. Stand firm on things like safety, nutrition, discipline and television, but give your nanny a break when she changes the settings on the car radio.

- Take time to listen (easier said than done) and empathize (ditto).
- Be generous with money (pay her more than the cleaning woman, for God's sake) and time (it's only polite to call if you're going to be late).
- Be flexible about vacation schedules (who can blame a woman whose relatives live abroad for wanting to take off two weeks in a row?).

Happily, there are times when things fall into place even without your most noble efforts. One of those times for us last year was Halloween. I like to take that day off, because it's a major holiday in my family. It turned out to be beautifully convenient, in that October 31 was an important holy day for Kumarie's husband, a Hindu, and she had a big feast to prepare. So we gave her the day off.

Just a couple of working girls, dovetailing their schedules. It works like magic today, but I'll always remember the hard work it took. I'm proud of the relationship we've managed to craft over the past three years, and I expect Kumarie is proud too. In her way, she lets me know. The other morning, she told me, Erica looked around and asked, "Where's Mommy?" Kumarie replied, "Mommy's gone to work." And Erica said, "Oh, and you're here. I love you."

Tag, you're it.

Teach Your Daughters Well

by Sonya Friedman

If there's one lesson every mother should impart to her
daughter, it's surely this: To thine own self be true.

S itting around the deck of a luxury cruise ship last
spring, my seven longtime friends and I celebrated
our coming-of-age. Ranging from our early fifties
to our early sixties, we numbered six business-
women, a homemaker and me, a clinical psychologist. All of us had worked hard to whittle out two
weeks from busy schedules for a trip that was to be "womano a
womano," no men invited. This was not to be viewed as a rejection of men, we explained to our spouses; rather, it was an affir-
mation of ourselves at a time in our lives when we *could* travel
with our husbands but wanted the pleasure of spending time
with dear friends. We chose to be selfish, and it was so delicious!

Conversation went nonstop. We reflected on who we were in
our younger days and who we had become. We felt smugly
comfortable that we had acquired a great deal of information
about life over the years, that what we knew added up to a certain
amount of wisdom and that wisdom was meant to be shared and
passed from one generation to the next.

As we relaxed by the ship's pool and caught the last rays of
the Mediterranean sun, discussion turned to what our mothers

had told us about life and love. "What words of wisdom did your mother give you?" I asked each woman in turn. The silence was stunning.

"Can I get back to you on that?" Leslie inquired.

"My mother never told me anything," said Janet. "I guess I just watched the way she lived her life."

Given my profession, I goaded them to be more specific. Bits of folk wisdom began to emerge: "In case you're in an accident, always wear clean underwear." "Put away a little money for yourself; you never know when you might need it." Some remembered their mothers warning them about men who "just wanted one thing." But for most of us, the messages were another kind of warning: Find yourself a man as quickly as you can and get married. And then? A woman needs to give 80 percent, and a man, 20 percent, to make a marriage work. And then? If something went wrong, it was the woman's fault. She had failed, not he. In the main, the information was restrictive and reactive, intended by mothers to protect their daughters from life's events.

> Let's tell our daughters that choices have consequences that can't always be revised.

The pendulum swings wide. After thirty years in a practice specializing in problems of marriage and the family and having published five self-help books and conducted thousands of interviews on ABC talk radio and CNN's *Sonya Live*, I've seen numerous fad philosophies come and go. They range from Dean Martin singing "You're nobody till somebody loves you" to that oft-repeated slogan of the early 1970s: "A woman needs a man like a fish needs a bicycle." What many women want today appears to be a sense of total autonomy. But with this comes disconnection and loneliness.

Somewhere in between is a level of comfort that acknowledges the need for individuality while at the same time recognizing that men are a vital part of what is considered family life.

Sad to say, the women of my generation were not given messages that allowed them to feel that they owned their lives or that the world was theirs to conquer. The underlying statements were primarily about managing men. "Marry him first, then change him" was a frequent refrain. A successful woman was able to find a man who would give her what she could not give herself: a rewarding sense of accomplishment.

By dinner, my cruise mates and I all agreed that our mothers had not prepared us for the world we came to live in. Of the eight of us, only three are still in our first marriage; all but one have daughters. Had we done any better?

We spent the greater part of our lives becoming independent and cosmopolitan, a new breed of women after whom our daughters would model themselves. We gave them the sense that they could go into the world and try anything. We also gave them a sense of entitlement. They deserved whatever they wanted: great jobs, great marriages, great kids. They had choices most of us hadn't even known enough to dream about. They went after big careers, gave up Mr. Right to look for Mr. Perfect, and put off having children until their late thirties or until their careers were established.

With all of these choices, why did so many women in our daughters' generation turn out to be unhappy? Some lived their lives consumed with blind ambition. Work became all, and happiness meant getting to the top. Some gave up careers, because making a career of being a mother was more satisfying. They turned their lives over to their children and became slaves to them in an attempt to be perfect moms. Some went after the men they wanted with an impossible fury. Not able to wait for a boyfriend to call, they called him, took care of his needs, did his errands, then watched bitterly as he moved on. They were so busy saying yes, they forgot that *no* is the word that gives a woman her greatest power. Had we forgotten to teach our daughters that a man must work for her love?

What went awry on the information highway? If I were to start over with your daughter or mine and share what I now know, I told my friends, the message would be quite different. I'd tell her that while life is about choices, every gain breeds a loss. You cannot have a big-time career without putting your family second. You cannot be a career mom without suffocating your children; you need to pull back enough to keep a sense of self. The concept that you can have it all has shown itself to be a myth. It seems that we, who felt so put down, so limited in our options, lived out our unfulfilled desires and an apparent need for revenge through our daughters. And they run the risk of becoming unhappy when they cannot find the perfection of our dreams.

A whole generation of women exhausted themselves trying to have it all, when we should have encouraged them to examine the choices and pick out the ones that suited them best.

Did we put too much pressure on our daughters with that "you can be anything you want to be, reach for the top" attitude?

By telling them there were no limits, did we serve up impossible standards? Yes. They could marry late or not at all. They could elect to be childless and never apologize for it. They could divorce when the chemistry withered.

Instead, let's tell our daughters that choices have consequences that can't always be revised. Sure, you can change your mind along life's path, and doing so doesn't equate with failure or weakness. But the sooner you know who you are, the more you can trust your choices.

Most important, we must help our daughters to understand that they are responsible for the decisions they make. We must emphasize the importance of gaining control over emotions, of being open to criticism, of having a set of values and standards that they and those around them can live with. In selecting a mate, a woman must seek someone whose flaws she knows and can live with. (And someone who knows her flaws and can live with them too!)

In sum, I would pass this on to my daughter and yours: Know who you are and where you're going, and then find someone who wants to share your dream. And do it in that order.

VII
YOU MUST BE
KIDDING

Kindergarten Madness

by Christine Pittel

Getting your youngster into the right school is anything but child's play. How do you keep your sanity—and your civility?

Thn e phone rang in the admissions office of a top-drawer private school. "I think we've just conceived a child," the breathless caller said. "I want to put our names down on your waiting list." The presumptive parent may have been about three years and nine months premature, but he wasn't far off. For more and more families, the search for the right kindergarten and the lapses in good judgment that often attend it begin almost before the christening cup is engraved.

From start to finish, navigating the high-pressured process requires not only supporting but also protecting your child, virtually keeping him out of a loop that centers on him. Like a game, it asks parents to play fair but also to cultivate the ability to rush the net. Indeed, as the competition escalates for a seat around the table where the milk and graham crackers are served, both wing-tipped CEOs and baseball-capped dot-commers find themselves supplicants at the same door. Normally polite people can sometimes forget their manners.

In a way, the admissions process turns parents into children again: They feel vulnerable and subject to arcane rules and a higher, mysterious authority they don't quite understand. What used to be a simple rite of passage for children has also become a test of social skills for adults. Having recently embarked on this odyssey with our daughter, my husband and I know firsthand that the course bares you to the bone. It asks who you are and what you value, then gives you a glimpse of what the larger world values about you. For some, the exercise leads to a form of self-knowledge. Others, who don't quite get into the swing of one of America's most intricate social gavottes, are prone to missteps.

How do thoughtful parents avoid such slips?

You can start by acquainting yourself with the routine of the application dance. Generally, it begins with setting up a tour at the schools you're interested in (a frustrating exercise in New York, where busy signals can be endless in the first hours when schools begin scheduling tours). After you've narrowed your choices, you submit formal applications. That's followed by the all-important interview with the child and one or both parents. Months later, a thick or thin envelope arrives by mail.

If pretension is never attractive, it's particularly counterproductive when a child's future is at stake. A parent's first impulse may be to roll out credentials and inflate achievements, but discretion is the better part of social valor; it's more appropriate to maintain a certain modesty and restraint. If you've filled out the application deftly—distilling your appeal into a few strategic names and phrases—you've already put your accomplishments on the record. So you're free to mention your avocation as lead guitarist in a zydeco band or last year's voyage up the Sepik in Papua New Guinea. Your child's best asset is the best version of yourself you can gracefully be.

In the search for letters of recommendation, overreaching is epidemic as people grasp for the furthest tendrils of their social network. Pressuring people who are not your friends is a faux pas. Instead, present the request as an invitation so that it won't be awkward to decline. You'll melt at the kindness of some people—and bury the painful moments when you learn that others don't want to spend their hoarded chips on your child. "One or two well-placed letters that are genuine can help," says Melinda Kanter-Levy, executive director of the Marin Day Schools system in the San Francisco Bay area. "But bombarding a school with more can be too pushy." A letter from someone within the school community who really knows the family counts more than a drive-by celebrity endorsement.

The interview, with only a psychiatrist's hour to make an impression, calls for true grace under pressure. "Parents start off on the edge of their seats," says Elizabeth Krents, admissions director at the Dalton School in Manhattan. "I consider it a major achievement to get them to scoot back on the couch and realize they can relax and be themselves." Admissions officers are professional judges of character with antennas that can pick up messages radiated by a cuff link.

A poised delivery can make even the most prosaic message poetic, so prepare for that interview. Since bragging is always self-defeating, smart couples sometimes set up jump shots for each other; a boast becomes something else when one spouse is extolling the virtues of the other. But not everyone arrives with practiced teamwork. Admissions directors have seen it all: the elbow to the rib, the flaring arguments, the chill between estranged spouses (who should make separate appointments).

And stow that cell phone; if you can't control your cellular, how can you control your child? (One father, keen to prove just how involved he was in his child's life, breached common courtesy by making a play date over his phone *during* the interview.)

Savvy parents demonstrate proper consideration for the school by doing their homework and knowing its mission ahead of time. Each institution is a culture unto itself, with its own pedagogy and personality. Some moms and dads make the mistake of running on about how their child likes to line up every last diskette neatly on his desk when they're interviewing at a school that prides itself on free-form creativity.

Parents often wonder whether it's acceptable to make a donation to their school of choice during the admissions process. Definitely not. "We have even gotten applications with checks attached to them," says

> In a way, the admissions process turns parents into children again.

Laddie Dill, a trustee of the Crossroads School in Santa Monica, California. "It simply doesn't work that way."

Nor is it the time to become an overnight sensation on the civic circuit. "There's no need to scurry about trying to start five community-service projects just to fluff out your profile," asserts the Dalton School's Krents.

"We see right through that pretty quickly. I'm much more interested in hearing about how you hang around in your pajamas on Sunday mornings and cook breakfast together. I can feel when parents talk with passion about something they truly love."

Selecting and then courting the right schools amounts to a

multiple flirtation but shouldn't veer into promiscuity. It's bad form to tell more than one school that it's your first choice. (And even if ethics don't concern you, consider that there's also a chance you could be exposed; admissions directors do tend to converse with one another.) If you've asked a trustee to go to bat for you, etiquette dictates that you honor an acceptance should you receive one.

Acceptances, of course, are not the real test of grace. Administrators never hear from most people who receive a rejection letter, but a few of the more presumptuous parents are on the line right away—one hopes out of their child's earshot. (As for those on the waiting list, besieging the admissions office with daily telephone calls reveals a little too much about their regard for other people's time.)

If you have any experience with carefully laid plans that backfire, then you've learned not to pressure a four-year-old to perform. But something insidious happens when you receive that thin envelope with a letter beginning "We're sorry . . ." Someone else's evaluation of your child starts crowding out your own. You catch yourself looking at your youngster, and even at yourself, differently. It's as if you've been issued a report card on your own status in society, and nobody understands that the grade is unfair.

Most children will get into some schools but not others. Both outcomes demand diplomacy. Disappointed parents may sulk or take the high road and seize an opportunity to teach their children—by example—a lesson in good sportsmanship. And beyond practicing tact within the family, decorum is expected outside the front door as well: gloating is as impermissible as asking another couple where their child got accepted.

Way Too Familiar?

by Joan Caraganis Jakobson

Before your kids get too chummy around their elders, make sure they understand the importance of titles like Mister, Aunt, Grandpa and, yes, Mom and Dad.

A s I picked up my five-year-old son after a play date at his friend's house one afternoon, I reminded him to thank Mrs. Davis. "Oh, no," Mrs. Davis scoffed, "we don't like all that formality, all that Mr. and Mrs. stuff. Just call me Susie." She then turned to her own son, whom I had not met before, and said, "Say goodbye to Joan." I smiled weakly, resisting the urge to inform Susie that it was possible for children to be respectful without sounding overly formal. What Susie chose to do with her son was her decision, but the minute I was alone with my child, I informed him that, although there would be exceptions, generally speaking, he should not call adults by their first names until he, too, was a grown-up.

The current practice of children addressing adults by their first names has become distressingly commonplace. In the same way that many parents believe traditional schools stifle creativity, they're also convinced that traditional family labels act as an emotional restraint, that children's affections for people are hindered by formality. These mothers and fathers don't realize that traditions provide the security that gives their children the freedom to grow. In a world in which families are smaller and fractured by divorce, family members are isolated from one another, and parents must sometimes create a family for their children with friends rather than with relatives. In these circumstances, parents who discourage titles are unknowingly forfeiting a soothing connection for their children.

Clearly, these parents feel that in this casual era, asking their children to call all adult relatives and friends by their first names is the right thing to do. They have decided that familiar old titles like Grandma and Grandpa, Aunt and Uncle or Mr. and Mrs. are part of a meaningless, stodgy and confining tradition. But it is important that we raise our children to understand that not everyone is equal and that adults are worthy of a certain deference by virtue of their age. If we abandon the use of Aunt and Uncle and Grandma and Grandpa, we deny our young relatives an especially affectionate attachment to their family members, one that is just a bit harder to come by when those same people are referred to by their first names.

Imagine the effect that this oddly egalitarian situation might have had on a few fictional families of our past. If Patrick Dennis had written about a rather loud woman called Mame who drank a lot and either gave or went to a different party every night, it would have been reasonable to question her credentials for bringing up a young boy. But *Auntie* Mame? She sounds like the perfect person to protect and adore her young charge, buy him lots of books and teach him to dance.

Had Opie Taylor raced through the streets of Mayberry,

thrown open the door of his house and yelled, "Bee, I'm home!" he no doubt would have ended up working as a temp at the local bait-and-tackle shop. But Aunt Bee does indeed convey the impression of a loving woman who provided the young boy with a snug and carefree life.

Do we really want to live in a world without an Aunt Polly, an Auntie Em or an Uncle Sam? Isn't it possible that we might have lost World War I if our nation's young men had been forced to gaze at recruitment posters of a peculiarly dressed old chap named Sam who pointed a finger and exhorted them to register for the draft because "I want you"? (Nobody would have signed up, and we'd all be fluent in German, eating strudel served by Tante Magda.)

Although it might be gratifying to blame the media for the unsettling trend of dispensing with titles, it wouldn't be accurate or fair. Even on *The Simpsons,* young Bart calls his father by his first name, Homer, only at those moments when Homer is behaving like a clueless adolescent. During such exchanges, Bart has to become the parent and register his annoyance and disappointment. In the movie, *What Women Want,* Mel Gibson's teenage daughter refers to her father as Nick or Uncle Dad. She explains: "My father has always been like an uncle to me." Not until he stops dancing in his bathrobe to Frank Sinatra CDs and begins to take on the responsibilities of fatherhood does she finally call him Dad.

Many of today's grandparents recall dancing not to Ol' Blue Eyes but to Jefferson Airplane or the Rolling Stones. And since first names suggest youthfulness, any implied lack of respect on the part of the younger generation is of minor significance if

Grandma can still picture herself belting out "Hey! You! Get off'a my cloud" while wearing a peace-symbol pendant and white go-go boots.

My daughter's friend Samantha says, "I have two grandmothers. I call one Grandma, and the other one, well, what she wants me to call her changes constantly. First it was Granny; then, when she divorced her third husband, it was Maryanne; and now that she's gone to law school, it's Mimi." It sounds as if the Three Faces of Granny, in an effort to pretend that aging is not a part of life, are operating at the expense of Samantha, who just wants her grandmother back.

> The current practice of children addressing adults by their first names has become distressingly commonplace.

Familial titles can also be useful in stepfamilies. If genuine affection exists between a child and his stepfamily, the aunt and uncle designations can help to define those relationships. When a child calls his stepmother's siblings Aunt Helen and Uncle Peter, it's a lot more endearing than simply Helen and Peter. Of course, these relationships are not always so cozy. I called my chilly stepmother's equally indifferent siblings by their first names; the notion of addressing them by the same titles I used for the aunts and uncles who played a loving part in my life would have seemed misplaced at best.

In some families, nicknames can provide a special bond. My husband's college roommate, known to his friends as Dirty because of the state of his dorm room, his clothes and sometimes his language, is a beloved Granddirty to four children. A college friend of mine who spent many years living the hippie life in Santa Fe is now affectionately referred to as Granola by her grandchildren.

For youngsters, having a distinct appellation for those who are closest to them is not just a matter of etiquette but also one of emotional well-being. Dr. Antonio Beltramini, a child psychiatrist in New York City, says, "The family is the place where the drama of life is played out. In a society in which family ties are disappearing, it is important that children grow up with a sense of connection to their relatives. Calling relatives by their given names is a rejection of the fact that they are indeed connected; it blurs the family structure by denying relatives their roles."

Words will always float in and out of our lives; and it is precisely this fluidity that sustains our language. But there are some words that we shouldn't let go of without a fight. I think it's time that we reclaim these once treasured titles and return them to their rightful heirs. That would include the five-year-old nephew of a friend of mine, a boy who knew his aunt simply by her first name. One day he said to his mother, "Caroline is a nice lady, Mommy. Who is she?" Caroline, her nephew, and his generation deserve better.

It's Grand *and* Great

by Hugh Downs

After raising children and grandchildren,
the best is yet to come.

I'm having more fun being a great-grandfather than I had as a grandfather or a father, and I think I know why. (It is surely more than just my great-grandson's charm: Upon meeting a good-looking woman, he is apt to take his Binky out of his mouth and offer it to her.)

Alexander William Black was the first true newborn I ever saw. (My children were cleaned up and a half-hour old before I was allowed near them. And for geographic reasons, I did not see either of my grandchildren until they were weeks old.) But I met Xander, grandson of my daughter and son of my grandson, seven minutes after he was born. The door to the delivery room was opened for us, and his two grandmothers and my wife, Ruth, and I went in.

Xander was red and wrinkled and protesting loudly against being thrust into the harshness of this world. In a few weeks he was a personality to Ruth and me, and in exactly twelve months he proved himself a biped: He toddled. Shortly after that he began to experiment with running. Fifty percent of his excursions ended in crashes, but he did not give up and now, at twenty months, he runs formidably.

Left alone with him when he was a month old, I had to prepare his bottle and change his diaper. In addition to marveling at the advances in diaper technology since my children were little, I reflected on the fact that I hadn't changed a diaper in more than half a century and that one was on this child's grandmother—my daughter.

Parenting is on-the-job training. In spite of a lot of the advice in magazine articles and TV segments—perhaps more than we should be subjected to—there is virtually no real education for baby rearing. By the time you have acquired the skills and wisdom to be a good father or mother, your children have grown up and moved away.

So you become a grandparent, and finding yourself now fit to raise children, you also realize that they are not yours. You have the skill but not the authority; the parents are in charge. This can be seen as a plus, since you probably don't want full-time responsibility; you've been through that. It's nice to be able to return the little ones at the end of a babysitting session. But the quality of time with them is somehow greater than that enjoyed during full-time parenting.

Becoming a great-grandparent is a whole new ball game. Your grandchildren, remembering with fondness what you were to them, regard you with affection and gratitude for being willing to sit with their progeny and impart some of your wisdom. (Age alone can sometimes spawn enviable respect.)

But there are other dimensions that make the job far more glorious than the previous steps of ancestoring: the added maturity of moving from "grand" to "great" allows a deeper glimpse into the mystery of how a child grows (and why). What I remember of my own childhood had increased meaning while I watched my children grow. My grandchildren reinforced this outlook. And now, a great-grandchild has locked in these harmonies and given them the cache of long-loved music that has a harmonic "rightness." The wisdom does not come in the form of answers to questions but rather in the beauty of knowing the right questions to ask.

Xander is our flesh and blood. But my wife and I each contributed only 12.5 percent of his DNA. He has six other great-grandparents. And while we see traits and features of ourselves in him, they are fainter, for his character and features are those of humanity. Somehow this makes him even dearer, and it is through him that we move closer to understanding how much of a family we all are, kin to every other human being on the planet.

> A great-grandparent can teach the necessity of sharing, compromise, obedience and patience.

He is, of course, unique. After Xander found his belly button, he had to investigate the belly buttons of each of his parents and other living ancestors, including Ruth's and mine. A young girl who is a friend of Ruth's recently got too near him, and he lifted her T-shirt to scout whether she was endowed with a navel. I never thought of this technique when I was pursuing young females. (Let's keep him under close surveillance.)

It helps to have compressed generations in one's background. My father was scarcely twenty-one years older than I; I had a family of my own in my early twenties; my daughter was married in her teens—this is what allows me to enjoy a great-grandson who will be out of infancy when I'm still in my early eighties.

I'm grateful for this. And grateful to his parents, who indulge Ruth and me in the time we want with him. Watching him grow and learn and sometimes just seeing his face when he is asleep bring us close to tears.

I suppose one element in the pride of having this delightful young fellow in our lives reflects the pride we have in ourselves for having helped in his production. And pride in sixty years of marriage and in having established, without any self-caused disasters, a fully functional family: two children, two grandchildren, and now a new layer with a new family graciously allowing us to fit in.

Being an ancestor is a great honor, and it carries much responsibility. The responsibility comprises being a role model, trying to ease the bumps of disappointment and frustration that the very young inevitably encounter and cushioning the shock and devastation for a firstborn on learning when a sibling arrives that the center of attention shifts to a different person. A great-grandparent can also teach the necessity of sharing, compromise, obedience and patience. We come into the world not needing to learn how to breathe or swallow or cry or excrete. But almost everything else has to be learned, and this is a chance for great-grandparents not only to log quality time for themselves but to shine among other relatives, including doting grandparents.

What better occupation could I have—have I ever had—than to offer this child whatever energy, time and substance I have left toward enhancing his chances in the world? To answer his questions when I can, to share adventures with him and to be a part of the scaffolding from which he and his parents seek to build his life.

There are many great-grandparents in the human community, and I'm sure most of them have the same emotions and intentions Ruth and I have. The young are better at reproducing, but the best of them are merely equal to the old in nurturing.

We are delighted that Xander arrived before we left. We intend to watch him grow. If we enjoy enough longevity to see him grown, we will qualify as truly venerable elders.

And I don't see anything wrong with that.

VIII
HOME IS WHERE THE HEART IS

Respectful Renting

by Stacey Okun

A bit of consideration can spell the difference between
a memorable experience and a miserable one.

I t's a lazy summer afternoon in the Hamptons. The sun
is glistening on the pool; the sunflowers in the garden
seem to be growing taller by the moment. My two little
boys, tanned and barefoot, are on the swings, so happy
to be here that they've temporarily forgotten their
rivalry. I am on the back porch, sprawled in my
Adirondack chair, thanking my lucky stars for this paradise: my
beautiful summer home, my beloved town of Bridgehampton,
my sunflowers. But, I must confess, they are not exactly mine.
Just mine for the summer. When Labor Day comes around, I will
leave this place spotless and, I hope, without a trace of our ever
having inhabited this house, this land, for four months (lest the
real owners take a chunk out of our security deposit).

Like thousands of Americans from Martha's Vineyard to
Malibu, my husband and I rent a vacation house each summer.
Living in someone else's home—taking naps on some other
family's hammock, flying someone else's American flag on the
Fourth of July, and, yes, sleeping in someone else's bed (although
I always bring my own bedding, right down to the pillows)—
lends an intimacy to the situation that I find difficult to disregard.

Thus, I have never been able to consider this transaction "just business." Handling this relationship well, on both sides, can literally mean the difference between a good and a bad summer. Yet, despite the work that goes into the landlord-tenant relationship, my husband and I keep going back.

With two kids, a nanny, and a steady stream of (mostly) welcome houseguests, we like our rental homes spacious and sophisticated—an extension, albeit a more countrified one, of our home in the city. But this preference is exactly what makes renting a prickly subject: the nicest homes belong to owners who care about them, who've decorated them with love and given them character and who are probably more than a little reluctant to leave them. They do leave, however, and more than likely are financing their own summer getaways with the proceeds from ours.

So what does sometimes happen when the owner moves out and the tenant moves in? "Oh boy, could I tell you some horror stories," says Peggy Griffin, principal managing director and a partner of Allan M. Schneider Associates in Bridgehampton, New York. She estimates that 12 percent of the company's business last summer was in luxury rentals. Griffin regales me with tales of rude renters who dried marijuana in the basement and of others with big, shaggy, shedding, slobbering dogs in tow who gleefully dug up all the shrubs. Equally offensive at times can be the homeowners themselves. "A few years back we rented a fabulous beach house to a famous artist who prefers not to be named," Griffin recalls. "When he showed up on the first day, the house was filthy." A rush cleaning job, funded by Allan M. Schneider, saved the day—and the summer.

To help save your summer, I've prepared the following tips:

As the Landlord, You Should . . .

- Without question, leave the tenant an immaculate house. Personal belongings you don't want the tenant to use should be locked in the attic or in one large closet, but everything that is left out (e.g., the grill, the patio furniture, the kitchen accoutrements, the digital alarm clock) should be in good working order, ready to use.

- Provide a list of important contacts and their telephone numbers on the kitchen counter. The list should include the plumber, electrician, caretaker or fix-it man, pool-maintenance service, gardener, local phone and cable companies, garbage-pickup service and all emergency numbers.

- Discuss in advance all bills for house services, such as who pays for the gardening from May through September.

- Take the renters on a tour of the house, teaching them how to work everything from the pool heater to the stereo system to the burglar alarm. Those extra few minutes are likely to cut down on repairs.

- Never drop in unannounced. If you must stop by, have the rental agent call ahead so your tenants know when to expect you.

- Avoid excess phone calls, especially ones that go something like this: "How are my hydrangeas doing? Are you sure you know how to use the electric awning . . . do you want me to stop by and run through it again? You are bringing the pool cushions in when it rains, aren't you?" Understand that once the tenants move in, the house is theirs until the lease says it's not.

- Be responsive if things do go wrong. One of our landlords didn't seem to have an ounce of concern for his beachfront home once he left. Early in the summer, the front doorknob started sticking, making it difficult to enter the house. We called to ask him how he wanted us to proceed with the repair, and we got no response. Within a month we were kicking in the door like detectives from *Law & Order* until Griffin, our pint-size broker, finally fixed it herself.

- Return the security deposit in due time. Once the landlord has assessed the damages incurred over the summer and the last round of bills have all been settled (in September), the remainder of the security deposit should be returned without delay.

> Living in someone else's home lends an intimacy to the situation that I find difficult to disregard.

As the Tenant, You Should . . .

- Advise the landlord beforehand if you are bringing your own belongings to the rental, so that he can store dishes and bedding away neatly and carefully before your arrival.

- Get permission prior to move-in day for the installation of anything that might mar the property, such as swing sets (they make holes in the grass) and childproof pool gates (which can make holes in cement or brick decks).

- Find out how the landlord wants his phone calls fielded and politely direct all callers to those numbers.

- Take care of the landlord's belongings. Some wealthy renters I know in Newport, Rhode Island, take an "I'll pay for it if it breaks" attitude toward their rentals. A more respectful approach: If you wouldn't let your two-year-old ram her Little Tikes convertible into *your* wood coffee table, don't let her do it to someone else's.

- Be honest. If the lease says no pets, don't sneak your black Lab, who sheds and drools and eats rattan porch furniture for breakfast, into the house. One Water Mill, New York, landlord visited (with permission) her home during the summer and was surprised to find a cat sitting smack in the middle of the kitchen table. "That's no pet," the tenant informed the piqued landlord. "That's Bessie. She's our third child."

- Disclose damages. I routinely end each summer with a brief phone call to the landlord as well as a note left on the kitchen counter listing damages.

- Finally, leave the house in immaculate condition. Discard anything you don't want to bring home. Don't leave remnants of the last cookout on the grill. Don't leave dried Play-Doh stuck like glue to the deck (guilty as charged). Don't leave your children's neon-hued turtle-shaped pool floats piled up in the outdoor Jacuzzi. Do leave some detergent in the laundry room, toilet paper in the bathrooms (as you would hope the landlord did for you) and flowers in the garden (don't go on a cutting spree the last day of your lease).

As I near the completion of this essay, my husband and I have just signed the lease on what we think may be our last rental house. It might soon be time to build our own dream home and take on all the responsibilities of creating and caring for it. But my newest and perhaps nicest landlord made me realize what I will miss most about renting. "We've had so many happy times in this house," she said, describing the home she was entrusting to my family for the season. "There's a good aura here. You should enjoy it. And besides, we've done all the work for you. All you have to do is relax."

In the Company of Friends
by Karen Duffy

A guide to getaways with close companions.

For the past several years, my husband and I have rented a large villa on Mustique. It's like paradise, the perfect escape from our lives in Manhattan. Yet beyond the lure of its idyllic beaches and brilliant sunsets, what we most look forward to about our annual trip to the Caribbean is that we are joined by several of our closest friends.

Travelers accustomed to intimate getaways might shudder at the thought of spending their holiday with two or three other couples. However, there are significant advantages to sharing a vacation home. From a practical standpoint, it allows us to pool our financial resources. With rentals for a first-rate villa going for around $20,000 per week, sharing enables us to secure a larger home than we could on our own. Indeed, the house we rent resembles the lair of a James Bond villain. It is a fully staffed, over-the-top estate with mesmerizing views. It has four bedrooms, three pools, waterfalls, koi ponds, lush tropical gardens, a billiard room, a fully equipped gym, a media room, a hot tub, numerous balconies, decks, sitting areas and an expansive main gallery for entertaining.

As exciting as it is to rent a *Dr. No* abode, an even nicer benefit is that we get to spend expanses of quality time with people we love. When we're in New York, it seems that dinners and cocktail parties are the only chances we get to see our friends. By their very nature, such gatherings rarely allow the time for long catch-up sessions.

Mustique is the perfect place to relax with old friends. In contrast to some other Caribbean islands, it is very serene, an ideal getaway for our coterie of type-A New Yorkers.

For all of its appeal, sharing a vacation property with close companions does take work. The following are some of the lessons I have learned along the way, all of which grease the wheels of courtesy in a communal living situation:

- The main responsibilities my husband and I share as host and hostess are to coordinate the rental of the property and to determine which friends to share the house with. This process entails a bit of science—and diplomacy. Yet, to my way of thinking, creating the right mix of people is even more important than selecting the right house.

- Once we have decided whom to include, we send a written invitation with information on the island, photographs of the house, rental dates and, of course, the prices: house rental fees and approximate costs for food, liquor and telephone. If it is not handled properly, entering into a financial agreement with friends can end up costing you your friendship as well as your money. A letter that spells out all the details allows each couple to consider carefully the costs involved before deciding to join.

- About a week before your departure, it is a good idea to host an informal dinner for the houseguests. The gathering will provide an opportunity for everyone to meet and to discuss logistics, supplies and the menu. After you have decided on your meals, you should fax the list to the rental agent. Then, when you arrive, the grocery shopping will have been taken care of and the chef will have an idea of how your group prefers to dine.

Last year, two of our friends shipped ahead a case of very special wines and a selection of their favorite gourmet items from New York. When the group arrived, the wine was chilled and the on-site staff had prepared a reception with the gourmet items. It was a generous, thoughtful gesture.

- Before arrival, you should also consider where everyone will sleep. Our house accommodates each of the four couples with a private suite that includes a bedroom, dressing area, bathroom, sitting room and balcony with spectacular views. The communal areas are open and spacious, so guests can comfortably socialize or retreat into a quiet corner. This design also allows each couple to enjoy their own manner of relaxation.

- Be wary of running the holiday like a cruise director. Your job is to rent the house and fill it with friends. Be gracious, but allow your housemates to structure their own time. You are not responsible for everyone's entertainment.

- Running a large house efficiently with eight guests entails continual housekeeping, laundry, grocery shopping and meal preparation and presentation. Since my definition of a vacation is liberation from domestic responsibilities, the house we rent is fully staffed with a butler, a chef, two housekeepers and two gardeners. The less any of the guests have to worry about cooking and cleaning, the better.

The duty of overseeing the daily chores is in the remarkably capable hands of the staff, with whom we have established bonds over the years. Mr. Mickey Pearson, the butler, is charming, discreet and dedicated to giving us the most wonderful two weeks of our year. Josh, a terrific chef and the best tennis player on the island, surprises us daily by preparing thoughtful and unforgettable meals. He even bottles his homemade jerk sauce and orange marmalade for us to take home. Together with their team, Mickey and Josh run an immaculate and welcoming house.

This being a communal experience, there are also guidelines for guests:

As exciting as it is to rent a Dr. No *abode, an even nicer benefit is that we get to spend expanses of quality time with people we love.*

- Good manners equal a good vacation. When four couples share a house, there is no extra room for short tempers.

- Respect your housemates' privacy. Never enter a bedroom without permission, and be considerate of each individual's personal routine.

- Be aware of how your behavior affects the group. For example, if other guests dress for breakfast, you should also.

- Finally, remember to pitch in, whether that means going to the fish market, dropping off friends at the tennis court or planning a picnic.

Sharing a house with good friends will be an experience you will always remember. You are guaranteed good times, lots of laughs and sometimes a surprise or two. This year, for our last night on the island, some of our housemates planned a dinner party on the beach. They arranged for tables, candles, music and tiki torches to be set up on the sand. Once we sat down, the staff served us an amazing dinner. As we looked up at the stars, there was a single thought that enabled us to bear the prospect of going home the following morning: only fifty more weeks till our return.

Guess Who's Coming to Dinner?

by Jamie Lee Curtis

Surprise! It's you and your kids, carving out
quality time for supper.

The concept of family dinner often evokes a sense of nostalgia for a simpler time. Dad's job was to go out and earn a living while Mom stayed home and cleaned the house, washed the clothes and prepared a well-balanced, perfect food-pyramid meal complete with a Betty-Crocker-would-be-proud dessert for the family.

I'm not sure if that dream was ever reality. Growing up as the daughter of two Hollywood stars, I certainly did not live in a *Leave It to Beaver* world. My parents, both of them working actors, divorced when I was four, and my mother later remarried. To explain my childhood in a comic-book context, I was a Veronica but longed to be a Betty. And yet, if the quintessential nuclear family that takes time out for dinner each evening was an elusive ideal for people forty years ago, it's all but extinct today. In the modern era, Mom and Dad rush home from work to eat a few quick bites with the kids before heading out to a social function or a meeting. Other nights, everyone is so busy with various activities that dinner begins to resemble a game of musical chairs.

Each person winds up reheating leftovers on his or her own timetable or the family orders takeout before everyone rushes off to do something "more important."

We all can generate a list of reasons why we cannot possibly fit dinner with the family into our schedules. But the time has come to say enough with the excuses. Trust me, it means even more to your kids' futures than you might think.

Being a mother is the most important thing I do, and I am engaged in my children's lives probably more than they want me to be. I know that the habits I instill in my children will stay with them for life and that they will see the value, reap the benefits and continue these traditions with their own families one day.

> There is nothing more important than how you raise your kids and how involved you are in their lives.

As a result, I sit down to dinner with my kids every night. That's not to say that hectic work routines (both mine and my husband's) and the many activities of our kids (ages nine and nineteen) don't encroach on the sanctity of our mealtime. Fortunately, I was blessed to inherit my mother's outstanding organizational skills. That surely makes balancing career and family much easier.

One additional responsibility that I juggle is a seat on the board of the National Center on Addiction and Substance Abuse (CASA) at Columbia University in New York City. One of CASA's goals is to get parents to eat meals with their children. In a 2003 back-to-school survey of 1,987 adolescents ages twelve to seventeen, CASA determined that teens who ate dinner with their families five or more nights a week were at half the risk of starting to smoke, drink or use drugs. The teens were also twice as likely to get As in school as the teens who dined with their families two nights a week or less. This concept is mind-blowing, yet so simple.

To promote its mission, CASA has designated the fourth Monday in September as Family Day, a national reminder—similar to Mother's Day—for all of us to stay involved in our children's lives. According to CASA's founder and chairman, Joseph Califano, a U.S. Secretary of Health, Education and Welfare under Jimmy Carter, "Parent power is our most potent and underused tool in the campaign to prevent teen substance abuse."

Eating meals with their kids is something all parents can do, regardless of race, gender, family structure or socio-economic status. If, for whatever reason, a family dinner is impossible, consider a family breakfast, lunch or brunch—you get the picture. The beauty of this ritual is that there is no magic formula. Meals can be home-cooked or eaten in a fast-food restaurant. Involve the whole family in the plans. Pick an easy menu that will please all palates, and prepare the meal together. Let your kids choose what they want to eat or, if you don't cook, where they want to eat. Rotate the position of menu planner each week.

When my own family sits down for dinner, I am just plain "Mom" to my kids. My cooking is subject to the same complaints and criticisms that other mothers hear, but I welcome them. At least we're together and communicating.

I recommend starting the family-dinner habit when your kids are young, before all the external demands of life factor in. You can expand the formula from there, possibly making Tuesday ice-cream-sundae night or Sunday the time for a pancake breakfast. Keep mealtimes interesting by putting conversation topics into a hat and have each family member pick one and moderate a discussion around that topic.

Regular family gatherings encourage parent-child communication, which must be a priority for parents, no matter how busy they are. Making it a point to turn off the TV, ignore the phone and just spend quality time together is crucial to helping your children feel emotionally, spiritually and mentally balanced.

I have learned that there is nothing more important than how you raise your kids and how involved you are in their lives. It is our duty as parents, and I take this duty very seriously. And if I can find the time to have meals with my family, so can you.

IX
HOLIDAY CHEER

Let's Make a Meal

by Francine Maroukian

Even if the stuffing is gloppy and the sweet potatoes
are burned, Thanksgiving has a way of bringing out
the best in all of us.

I t might lack the up-in-lights star power of Christmas
or the drama of New Year's Eve, but for many people
(including myself) Thanksgiving reigns as their
favorite holiday. Late on Thanksgiving eve—the
best night of the year in New York as far as I'm
concerned—I walk around the dark, half-empty/
half-full city, and it seems so still. But it's out there. I can *feel*
Thanksgiving coming, the electricity and excitement converging
like the perfect storm. I know that in a few hours the entire town
will be swept up in the festivities. And when the day is over, I
never feel let down, because as good as everything was, the best
is yet to come (I'm talking leftovers).

According to my own unscientific poll, Thanksgiving is
universally enjoyable because it is a nondenominational national
holiday that by its very nature diminishes some of the conflicts
that can arise in our multicultural, interfaith families. Without
specific religious connotations (other than counting our blessings),
Thanksgiving is at liberty to be a more democratic, inclusive
celebration—a holiday whose heart is in the right place.

The spirit of the day doesn't manifest itself in the exchange of sheepskin gloves or cashmere scarves. Rather, at this particular observance, we are inspired to give of ourselves. Some of us invest time and money to return to hometowns that seem much smaller than the ones we left behind. Others express their seasonal urge to go home by re-creating Thanksgiving as they experienced it in days gone by and then sharing that version with friends (admittedly with a little less arguing and much better wine).

Having been catering director of New York's Silver Palate food shop in the early 1980s and later a private caterer, I've seen more than my share of Thanksgivings. During the weeks leading up to the fourth Thursday in November, my life was devoted to taking orders from customers who not only wanted food but were eager to talk about it—what they loved and what they hated, but mostly the private food moments they recalled from Thanksgivings past. As customers took turns rhapsodizing about Mom's defrosted supermarket turkey, I mentally replayed my own favorite holiday scene, from the 1970 film version of Sue Kaufman's book *Diary of a Mad Housewife.* Tina Balser (Carrie Snodgrass) pores over cookbooks to come up with a gourmet Thanksgiving menu that she hopes will complement the social-climbing needs of her pretentious husband (played by Richard Benjamin). Ultimately, both he and their children refuse to eat the meal, on the grounds that the oysters in the stuffing are "icky."

In my nearly three-decades-long catering and food-writing career, here is the most valuable lesson I have ever learned, and you can have it for free: there is an emotional charge to the Thanksgiving meal, and people count on familiar dishes. Even the most sophisticated palates—those who usually shun anything that isn't locally raised or regionally harvested—often crave the food they remember from their parents' table, right down to the omnipresent quivering cranberry roll, perfectly proportioned by the indentation of the rings inside the can.

Take it from someone who has been on both sides of the table: it's less about the food than the fellowship. To poach Thoreau, don't fritter away your day by obsessing over details. No one (at least, no one worth sharing Thanksgiving with) really cares if the piecrust is crooked or the napkins don't match.

Over the years, I have also come to respect and rely on the collective energy of Thanksgiving to carry me through. At no other time are so many of us planning, shopping and cooking for, and then eating, basically the same meal. When I was a private caterer, responsible for providing my favorite clients with all their turkey "fixings," there were times when I questioned the sanity of cooking in such quantity. But one look at the other market baskets during my shopping expeditions always made me feel much better; we're all in this together.

Even the fact that Thanksgiving is a big, time-consuming meal to prepare works to our advantage. There are always too many pots wrangling for space on too few burners, and every available inch of counter space is in use. But the chaos can be part of the coziness. Guests feel comfortable enough to wander in and out of the kitchen, asking when it will finally be time to eat, and cooks have no qualms about saying, "Here, stir this."

Another welcome expression of community is that Thanksgiving is not a time for couples only. One year I went out alone to the Regency Hotel on Park Avenue. Having a drink in the library lounge before dinner, I met a sixtysomething couple from Rockford, Illinois, and a trio of fellow New Yorkers. All of us strangers decided to meet in the lounge after we ate, and when we did, we pushed a few tables together and spent an hour drinking coffee and planning the out-of-towners' upcoming New York activities. Thanksgiving has the power to make families of us all.

For many, that feeling of kinship can also result in a day of good work, and I have been on the thanks-giving and thanks-receiving end of such generosity. A frequent guest at homes where the Thanksgiving table has graciously been extended to include "spares," I have also spent the day volunteering in an experimental, nonprofit restaurant in downtown Manhattan, greeting and seating customers. After the last patron had gone, I ate turkey with my coworkers, the aspiring cooks and waitstaff who were learning the restaurant business as part of an urban job-training program, every single one of them thrilled and proud to have played a part in producing such a tasty and important meal.

No one (at least, no one worth sharing Thanksgiving with) really cares if the piecrust is crooked or the napkins don't match.

Although preparations can create a kitchen free-for-all, there is still something quite civilized about Thanksgiving. We can count on it to be like the best houseguest, arriving exactly when it's supposed to. It doesn't slide around the week like Christmas or New Year's, which require frenzied planning as we juggle our work schedules and negotiate extra days off. For most of us, Thanksgiving is a four-day weekend, our official kickoff to the holiday season. Decorations are fresh, and so are we.

When we add it all up—the cooking and eating and freedom to create our family wherever we find it—what we get is a less intimidating, more relaxed holiday. Even those of us who occasionally fall under the lure of glossy food magazines somehow don't succumb to lifestyle envy at Thanksgiving. We might flip through the pages, admiring the artfully set tables, but when the pathological perfectionist in us raises its flawlessly groomed head, we know enough to stop it short with a well-placed truth: Thanksgiving is about keeping it real. And for that, let us all give thanks.

Playing Our Cards Right

by Andy Rooney

This year, resolve to send the rarest of Christmas greetings,
one that belongs on the mantel and not in the trash bin.

One of our culture's most civilized customs is the annual exchange of Christmas cards. We make more friends in our lives than we have time to keep, and Christmas cards provide a bridge to an enduring relationship. Most of these paper greetings fit into one of several categories.

There is the Early Bird. These come from friends who are so annoyingly well organized that they mail theirs before you have chosen yours. Millions of cards—the majority—read simply, "Merry Christmas and Happy New Year." I have often wondered why the phrase is not "Happy Christmas and Merry New Year."

The card slipped into your mailbox by the mailman, the trash collector or the newspaper delivery person in early December invariably falls short on genuine warmth. If you fail to respond with a twenty-dollar bill in an envelope, you get another message, reading "MERRY CHRISTMAS—SECOND NOTICE."

Even more impersonal are the Christmas cards from a company that has your name on file and barely conceals the sales pitch with a prefatory "Holiday Greetings!" No one wants "Holiday Greetings" coupled with an offer of a loan with no interest due until May. Neither are we interested in an aluminum-siding company's pretense of interest in our merriment at this time of year.

Last Christmas I was initially curious about a lovely card that showed an old farmhouse painted an attractive yellow. Its roof was covered with snow, as were the two barns behind it. I looked at it for a minute, enjoyed it and opened it up. "HAVE A WARM AND WONDERFUL HOLIDAY," it said. It was signed "FAIRFIELD COUNTY ALARM SERVICE, INC." Couldn't they at least have omitted the "inc."?

A family photo accompanies many of the cards I receive. A particular kind of friend sends these, and they are often interesting to inspect for evidence that the friends are aging more quickly than I am.

In recent years, thousands of people have sent cards that benefit the United Nations Children's Fund and say simply, "Peace." These cards are attractive and most often are from serious friends. While the sender has good intentions, Christmas cards with these messages do not seem to have had much effect on either peace or goodwill. It is furthermore a mistake to use Christmas cards for any propaganda purpose, even so good a one as UNICEF.

Then there are mystery cards. They are signed clearly "Jane and Bill," but Jane and Bill who? We have no idea. Making these mystery cards even more cryptic is that they usually arrive from a small town in the Midwest with a return address such as 3107 Maple Avenue. You would not offhand think that a town too small to be included in any atlas has a street with 3,106 houses on it before you get to the one owned by Jane and Bill. When these cards arrive in the mail, it is most usual for the husband to assume Jane and Bill are friends his wife sees in her investment club. The wife dismisses them as business friends of her husband's. It is not until they discuss it later—if they discuss it at all—that they find neither knows who Bill and Jane are or why that couple is trying to force the assumption of friendship on them. These cards can be very intrusive. When people who are fringe acquaintances force their way into the goodness of a genuine association, they diminish the significance of fellow-feeling for real friends.

> No one wants "Holiday Greetings" coupled with an offer of a loan with no interest due until May.

There are certain card-sending rules that we all observe. For example, if you mail a card to someone and don't get one in return, it is dangerous to skip him the following year, because he will almost certainly feel guilty about getting one from you and will put you back on his list. The Christmas-card exchange involves a two-year cycle. If you still don't receive a card after the second Christmas, having sent one to somebody for the previous two years, it is acceptable to remove him from your greeting-card roster.

When anything becomes as popular as Christmas cards are, commerce rears its ugly head and turns them into a crass business. Not surprisingly, the greeting-card industry hasn't always served Christmas well. In its effort to sell cards to everyone, it has made cards that are in worse taste than sour milk. There are cards in stores this year saying "Merry Christmas to My Wife" and "Merry Christmas to My Husband." A spouse who dispatches one of these is involved in a marriage that is not likely to last until next December 25.

There will often be several cards with little flaps representing a window on the front. They open to reveal a picture of a bearded Santa. Christmas cards should be in no way tricky or mechanical.

So, too, may a card be too cute. Christmas is not a day we associate with cleverness or humor. There is nothing somber about the day, but neither is it amusing, and cards should not suggest it is. Anything so elaborate is better saved for Valentine's Day.

And it is probably a mistake to send Christmas cards with a picture of Christ. It is pretty much conceded that Jesus was not born on December 25, and, because no one knows what he looked like, the rendition may be jarring when it doesn't match our own image of him.

For some time the religion-neutral "Happy Holidays" irritated me. It is, after all, a Christian holiday. I have not only become accustomed to "Happy Holidays," but I now prefer it. Christmas has become a time of year associated with friendship, family, warmth and goodwill toward all. It exceeds the boundaries of any one religion.

For this one wonderful day, we set aside our skepticism. We set aside our competitiveness. We set aside our ability to make logical decisions and we just hang around, relax, love one another, open presents and, yes, look at our Christmas cards.

Thank You for Not Sharing

by Andy Borowitz

There's nothing wrong with good tidings.
Just don't spread them with a holiday letter.

Decembr is a time of frenetic generosity. In the space of one month, we try to compensate for all our random acts of stinginess during the previous eleven. We dispatch crates of citrus fruits and frozen meats to people we wouldn't share a peanut with in the dog days of summer. And we succumb to the direct-mail appeals of charities that sound vaguely fraudulent, like the Fraternal Order of Librarians. We do all of this and more in a last-ditch effort to be generous or, failing that, extravagantly insincere.

But for some people, December generosity takes a different form. Convinced that the rest of us are tired of receiving oranges and flank steaks in the mail, they give the gift they believe we secretly crave: a full account of the amazing things that befell them, their family and their pets in the year just past. In this philanthropic spirit, these well-meaning but seriously misguided souls sit down to write their annual holiday letter, thus making our December journeys to the mailbox a study in dread.

No one knows precisely who wrote the first holiday letter.

Considering its durability as a literary form, surprisingly little scholarly inquiry has been devoted to its origins. Did William Shakespeare's mother whip out her quill to boast about her son's accomplishments? ("As for the little Shakespeares, 1599 has been a banner year! Billy's been hard at work on a super new play about the prince of Denmark, which we all know is just going to be his biggest smash yet!") Or do we have Mrs. Genghis Khan to thank? ("Genghis's job has kept him on the road too much this year, but he absolutely promises to take me to Europe in the spring!") It may be impossible to say when and where holiday letters began, but one thing can be said with total certainty: they must be stopped, and the sooner the better.

> As horrible as they tend to be, it's impossible to avert one's eyes from holiday letters, much like highway accidents.

Don't get me wrong. I've got nothing against the spectacle of a normally discreet person suddenly spilling personal information during the holiday season. On the contrary, when a senior partner has one vodka stinger too many at her law firm's holiday party and blurts out that she's leaving her husband for the pool man, I think that's entertainment at its best. But, sadly, most holiday letters have none of the festive charm of a good old-fashioned liquor-fueled confession. It's counterintuitive: given that they promise to pull back the curtain on their authors' personal lives, why aren't holiday letters more fun? Or, to put it another way, why are they such pure torture, worthy of prohibition by the Geneva convention?

First of all, the typical holiday letter tells much while revealing little, a classic bait-and-switch scam. The reason for this is simple: a holiday letter is the sanitized, official version of the author's year, usually written by someone with plenty to hide. This resolute killjoy has no intention of divulging any of the unsavory details we really care about or at least would stay awake for. Consequently, it's a mistake to read a holiday letter expecting to find juicy nuggets about sexual indiscretions or financial reversals that you can pass on to everyone in your e-mail address book. Most holiday letters are about as candid as an issue of *Pravda* at the height of the Cold War.

Shockingly, given their utter refusal to include even remotely interesting content, most holiday correspondents compound the tedium by making their letters unspeakably long. Burying the icky truth under an avalanche of inconsequential tidbits about triumphant tennis matches, glorious trips to the Vineyard and history-making family reunions where "a good time was had by all," some holiday letter writers can spew a narrative that makes Proust's *Remembrance of Things Past* look like an AOL instant message. Making matters worse, many of these once-a-year authors use their December letters as a bloated literary showcase for what they wrongly believe is their talent for puns, alliteration and (gulp) poetry. It all adds up to too much of a bad thing.

Reviewing my litany of complaints about holiday letters, some reasonable people might be tempted to ask why I read them at all, when I could just toss them away unopened, like those fund-raising letters I keep getting from the Al Gore Vice-Presidential Library. Well, easier said than done. If I threw them away, I'd live in mortal fear that I'd run into one of their authors at the mall or the dry cleaner, where, expecting me to be fully in the loop, he or she would lob an indecipherable conversation starter my way, such as "Well, I won't be ordering halibut in Luxembourg again anytime soon, huh?"

But there's another, more deep-seated reason why I don't throw them out. As horrible as they tend to be, it's impossible to avert one's eyes from holiday letters, much like highway accidents or the later films of Kevin Costner. Plus—and I know this will paint me as a rube—I keep hoping against hope that one day I'll actually receive an exception to the rule: a concise, riveting holiday letter that will make up for all the brain-numbing boredom of holiday letters past. What would it look like? Probably something like this:

Dear Friends,

The year 2002 was truly lousy, due mainly to the egregiously stupid decisions I made. I really have no one else to blame, much as I'd like to!

With my boorish and lazy behavior, I continued to alienate coworkers and superiors at an alarming rate. I wouldn't be surprised if they finally give me the ax next year, especially when they find out that I've been embezzling company funds and sleeping with the woman who waters the office ferns!

On the home front, Betty continues to spend money like a drunken sailor, and the resemblance doesn't end there. Incidentally, although she has told many of you that she had her appendix out in March, what she really had was a face-lift—her third this decade!

As for my children, they continue to be unremarkable and unimpressive in every way, with the possible exception of Kyle, who spent the past year in a maximum-security prison, where he can reasonably expect to stay for many years to come!

Oops, I see I've gone on too long!

Sincerely,
Your Friend,
the Irredeemable Loser

P.S. Don't send any gifts this year. In fact, you're off the hook forever!

The optimist in me says that someday I'll receive a gem like this in the mail; the realist tells me I'm kidding myself. But a man can dream, can't he? After all, crazy wishes are what the holiday season is all about. In the meantime, I'll soldier on, my eyes glazing over at the interminable accounts of successful bake sales, lacrosse trophies and miraculous recoveries from skiing injuries that this year's crop of holiday letters is bound to usher forth. But as I plow my way through the pile of epistolary sludge, I do have one consoling thought to cling to: December comes but once a year. Thank God.

Gifts That Go On Giving

by Tom Connor

The perfect present for a casual acquaintance might actually be very close at hand. (Too close?)

Things aren't going well at the mall. I've forgotten everything I ever knew about the people I'm shopping for: their likes and dislikes, quirks and characteristics, previous gifts I've given them. A passing group of gay men offers advice, but I'm apparently beyond help. (As they walk away, I hear one say, "He doesn't even know his wife's *colors*?")

Having taken weeks to get into the proper consumer spirit, I find it's suddenly Christmas Eve. Somehow, the only gifts left in the entire mall are ones that say "When you care the least and wait the longest to give the very worst." I buy them.

Actually, the big gifts for family and close friends have long since been scouted out, purchased, wrapped and tucked away in a closet. But it's the secondary presents—the filler, the stuff that boosts the gift count to socially acceptable levels—as well as the obligatory presents for neighbors and acquaintances, that I find the most challenging.

Judging by some of the things I've received for Christmases past, however, I'm not the only one handing out meaningless last-minute presents. Like the roommate of mine from college who once gave me a gift subscription to the Meat-of-the-Month Club. Or the red tie that looks as if, on the way home from shopping, its buyer (whose name on the card I'm still trying to decode) was attacked by Rottweilers and bled profusely.

I mean, why bother?

Exactly. For Christmas shoppers like me, the answer is *regifting,* that is, passing off as new a gift you've previously received. The term entered the cultural lexicon several seasons ago thanks to an episode of *Seinfeld* in which Jerry got regifted with a label maker.

For the regiver, at least, regifting can be a joyous and bountiful experience. First, it allows a person to shop from the convenience and comfort of his own home and at a very reasonable price: free. (This may not be good for the Economy, but it's good for my economy.) Another aspect of regifting is the concept of degifting, or ridding oneself of undesired gifts. Throw in unwanted birthday, confirmation, graduation and wedding presents, and you can stock your own Amazing Store!

While its benefits are obvious, what's surprising is how socially acceptable regifting has become. "It's permissible, but only with care," says Peter Post, great-grandson of Emily Post and a director of the Emily Post Institute. "You don't want to hurt the person who gave you the item by letting him find out that you've regifted it." (Technically, then, you could give my brother the very present I gave you last Christmas if, say, I were to sustain a mysterious injury and fall into a coma. Thanks, Peter.)

But Post has a point. Numerous occasions exist for which we receive gifts that not only will be untraceable but will benefit others more than they'll benefit us. Say you or I are invited to a party where the hostess hands out goody bags filled with imported foods and a pasta rake (something I once received). I don't know about you, but unless I were to wake up one morning to find my front lawn covered in vermicelli, I'd have no deep need for this item. Or it could be something you and I appreciate but probably would never use, like a perfectly good cologne or a nice-looking tote bag. What counts is that we give them to people we know will use them. What they don't need to know—and, more important, what they must have no way of finding out—is where the gifts came from.

Beyond that, a general sense of propriety informs several important dos and don'ts when regifting.

- Don't regift things you've opened and used, like soap or underwear, for instance, or chocolates you've tasted, such as a Whitman's Sampler with the jellied candies nibbled and replaced, bite side down, in the box.

- It should go without saying, but don't cross out your name on the original gift card and then write in the regiftee's. That's embarrassing for everyone. Remove the original gift tag.

- You can regift up a social notch or two by giving, say, the septic-tank man an '81 Pomerol (though why would you?); but a regift traveling in the opposite direction—like a pint of Old Mr. Boston blackberry brandy, wrapped in a brown-paper bag, for your hedge-fund manager—is probably going to leave a bad taste.

To that short list I should add a few don'ts of my own. Don't regift me: fruitcakes; self-help books or services for conditions I wasn't aware I had; cards designed to look like wallets and containing a fake, faded bill; or any Christmas-song collections by Pat Boone, Tha Dogg Pound, the Vatican All-Castrati Choir or Mariah Carey.

Most etiquette mavens decry giving away items that were handmade expressly for you. Are they serious? These are the kinds of gifts we most need to degift! Again, we must rely on our innate social sensibilities: what would be ruder, wearing a sweater with different arm lengths and revealing to everyone the name of the incompetent knitter or quietly passing it on?

The greatest regifting faux pas, according to Post, is giving others the very gift they gave you. Easy for him to say: he obviously never received a Chia Pet from a neighbor, as my wife and I did several years ago. It's the kind of gift that warrants not only degifting and regifting but an immediate response under a separate category that might be called retaliatory gifting: in other words, regift unto others as they would regift unto you. Far from awkward, however, this practice can lead to annually amusing situations in which the intentionally offensive gift goes back and forth, disguised in deceptive wrappings or hidden in unlikely places.

Much potential unpleasantness can be avoided by giving fair warning the moment you open a gift you know you'll be regifting.

"Of course I love it!" you might say. "Wouldn't *you?*" Or "You shouldn't have. No, I *mean* it."

Yet, should you find yourself confronted by someone who says "Wait a minute. Didn't I give you this very thing last Christmas?" only a direct answer will do. Simply reply: "Heavens, no. I would never give you something so tasteless. This is a *different* Hootie and the Blowfish T-shirt." Or, should push come to shove: "See? Doesn't feel so good when you're on the receiving end, does it?"

The greatest wish on my Christmas list this year is to receive so many thoughtless, tacky, pathetic, obviously last-minute gifts that I'll never have to shop again. I just hope they're not my own. And if they are, I hope I'll be gracious enough to accept them and simply say thank you.

FACE OF
THE NATION

X
HISTORY LESSONS

Speaking Presidential

Two centuries of life lessons from the
highest office in the land.

I n 1789, reviewing the expectant crowd gathered at
Federal Hall in Manhattan, a gentleman planter took
the oath of office as the first president of the United
States. His thirty-five-word vow, in which he swore to
"protect, preserve and uphold the Constitution," has
been uttered verbatim by each of the forty-two men
who have followed in his footsteps. Not all these leaders were as
memorable as George Washington. Nor have all of them been
gentlemen. Yet, whatever their failings and shortcomings, they
were statesmen who guided the nation through war and peace,
isolation and expansion, panic and prosperity. Each of them—
from "Honest Abe" Lincoln to Harry "Give 'Em Hell" Truman—
has added words of wit and wisdom to an invaluable American
patchwork. They have created an oeuvre filled with timeless
advice about how we should lead our lives as human beings and as
citizens. On topics from honesty to forgiveness, these are the
words that the world should note and long remember.

George Washington (1789–97) "Labour to keep alive in your
Breast that Little Spark of Celestial Fire Called Conscience"
[written at age sixteen].

Thomas Jefferson (1801–09) "When angry, count ten before you speak; if very angry, one hundred." • "Leave all the afternoon for exercise and recreation, which are as necessary as reading. I will rather say more necessary, because health is worth more than learning." • "In truth, politeness is artificial good humor. It covers the natural want of it, and ends by rendering habitual a substitute nearly equivalent to the real virtue."

John Quincy Adams (1825–29) "Courage and perseverance have a magical talisman before which difficulties disappear and obstacles vanish into air."

Andrew Jackson (1829–37) "One man with courage makes a majority."

Abraham Lincoln (1861–65) "This habit of uselessly wasting time is the whole difficulty; and it is vastly important . . . that you should break this habit." • "The sharpness of a refusal or the edge of a rebuke may be blunted by an appropriate story, so as to save wounding feeling and yet serve the purpose."

William McKinley (1897–1901) "That's all a man can hope for during his lifetime—to set an example—and when he is dead, to be an inspiration to history."

Theodore Roosevelt (1901–09) "No man is justified in doing evil on the grounds of expediency."

Woodrow Wilson (1913–21) "The world could dispense with high society and never miss it. High society is for those who have stopped working and no longer have anything important to do." • "I have always maintained that the man who lives to cultivate his own character will result only in cultivating an intolerable prig." • "The man who cannot change his mind gives evidence of profound ignorance . . . I'm willing to leave things alone if you will guarantee that I can go to bed and find them the same in the morning."

Calvin Coolidge (1923–29) "I have found in the course of a long, public life that the things that I did not say never hurt me."

Herbert Hoover (1929–33) "Despite the growing complexity of civilization, [the verities] stand out in simple concepts. They can be expressed as truth, justice, tolerance, mercy and respect . . . They can be expressed as sportsmanship, fair play, self-respect and good taste."

Franklin D. Roosevelt (1933–45) "Be sincere; be brief; be seated." • "If you treat people right, they will treat you right—ninety percent of the time." • "Motive in the long run is what counts—motive accompanied by good manners." • "Human kindness has never weakened the stamina or softened the fiber of a free people." • "Happiness lies not in the mere possession of money; it lies in the joy of achievement, in the thrill of creative effort."

Harry S Truman (1945–53) "Keep beating everyone in whatever you do, but be generous when you do it and don't make anyone feel badly when you beat him."

Dwight D. Eisenhower (1953–61) "But if each of us can feel he has done a little bit, whether it's a President trying to meet a crowd and make them believe that the United States truly wants peace, or whether it's a secretary who's always showing the courtesy and the politeness that some visitor expects, or if it's merely a good 'good morning' from an American as they pass someone on the street—I think this is one of the great jobs we can do outside, you might say extracurricular, because I know you are all busy."

John F. Kennedy (1961–63) "A man does what he must—in spite of personal consequences, in spite of obstacles and dangers and pressures—and that is the basis of all human morality." • "Only through the love that is sometimes called charity can we conquer those forces within ourselves and throughout all the world that threaten the very existence of mankind." • "Forgive your enemies, but never forget their names."

Lyndon Baines Johnson (1963–69) "Doing what's right isn't the problem. It's knowing what's right."

Gerald Ford (1974–77) "I like to give and I expect to receive or vice versa, but it is never in the sense of getting even."

Jimmy Carter (1977–81) "Saint Paul once said that the things that measure success and that never change are the things you cannot see. What are the things you cannot see? I would say justice and peace, humility, service, a willingness to forgive, compassion, sacrificial love. Those are the most important attributes of life."

> If you treat people right, they will treat you right— ninety percent of the time.

Ronald Reagan (1981–89) "The family is the best school of good manners and good behavior."

George H. W. Bush (1989–93) "It is in the daily accumulation of small acts of kindness that life can be improved."

Minding Miss Manners

Interview by Thomas P. Farley

Truths we hold to be self-evident.

Three times a week for the past twenty-five years, syndicated columnist Judith Martin has nudged humankind to clean up its act. After creating the "Miss Manners" concept for *The Washington Post* in 1978, she quickly became America's undisputed doyenne of good behavior, reaching readers of more than two hundred newspapers throughout North America and abroad. An eager public arbiter on quandaries of civility, she has also published two novels and eleven books, including *Star–Spangled Manners.*

Town & Country sat down with Martin at the historic Hay-Adams Hotel in Washington, D.C., where she offered her thoughts on the endurance—and evolution—of American etiquette.

How do you define manners, as opposed to etiquette?

Manners are moral principles, and they don't change. Etiquette comprises the surface rules that relate to a particular time and place and perhaps a subsection of society. Etiquette does change. People who think it's been static since Queen Victoria and I sat down and wrote it all out are sadly mistaken.

You probably feel that you'll never run out of rudeness issues to talk about.

If everybody behaved, I assure you, I'd be out on a porch hammock this very minute and enjoying it very much, but it is an ongoing task, yes.

People always talk about the decline of American manners. Do you think our manners have gone into a downward spiral?

[On the contrary], there's been enormous progress, particularly when we look at the treatment of women and minorities.

Allowing that there hasn't been a regression of etiquette in this country, do you ever feel that you're just working against a sea of horrible manners, that there's no way you can change the world?

There are times of discouragement, sure. But, fortunately, there are examples—September 11 and the immediate aftermath being one—that show the American people at their best. Every time there's an earthquake, a flood or a tragedy of some kind, the warmth, the helpfulness, the consideration, the kindness come pouring out.

Why, then, do Americans have a reputation for being ill-mannered?

I think there is a misunderstanding, a distrust of our openness, friendliness and lack of pretension. In theory, American manners are the best in the world. And the most influential.

What was the basis of American manners?

The Founding Fathers were all interested in etiquette, and

they wrote about it and they argued about it and there were some vicious congressional battles over how to turn etiquette as they knew it, which was stratified, into something that applied in an egalitarian society.

What was it about the people who founded this country that made them different from their counterparts in the Old World?

Some of them thought, "Here I can be the aristocracy," and others began to question the system that had let them down; [the latter group] prevailed. And I think it is very deeply ingrained here that everybody has to pull his weight. Anyone in this country who has inherited a lot of money but does nothing with his time is considered useless. Whereas in an aristocratic society at the time this country was founded, it was the opposite. If a wealthy person *did* do anything, he would be looked down on.

How did manners evolve after the founding era?

Well, they told us that "all men are created equal." Then we started questioning every word [of that phrase]. What does "created" mean? Do we all start at the same level, or do we have to help to make it more level? What do we mean by "all"? What do we mean by "equal"? Gradually, these things have been extended, and they're still being extended. The changes in the treatment of women and African Americans and lots of other groups are a work in progress.

So is "All men are created equal" the underlying theme of American manners?

Yes, if we could only decide what each of those words means.

It's a grand slogan, and it is the basis of American manners, although naturally it's subject to interpretation.

Is there a certain nostalgia about the old days, for a time when people were "so much better behaved" than they are today?

People who think that are thinking very selectively. While it's very nice [to look at pictures of] ladies in big hoop skirts, it's not so nice to realize that the skirts were covered with manure because the streets were knee-deep with it.

What about lessons that you'd like to see Americans learn from other cultures? People think of the English, for example, as being so well-mannered and charming.

In theory, American manners are the best in the world. And the most influential.

Well, they haven't been to England, have they? Look at British audiences at soccer games. They are much worse than American fans. Look at the institutionalized rudeness of putting people down, of refusing to talk to people, the lack of openness. There are a great many charming people in England, but to characterize England as a polite society when it lacks the helpfulness and openness to strangers that we have, when it lacks the crowd control, when it practices all kinds and forms of snobbery that are laughable here, that's not my idea of polite.

What are some of the manners that people cling to that they can finally let go?

"Ladies first" is drilled into a lot of people, and they do not understand it doesn't apply in all situations. In an elevator, for example, obviously the people in the front should get off first. And in the business world, gender is not supposed to be important. If you're going to jump to your feet, it should be for your boss.

What about chivalry in a nonwork setting?

I am not of the opinion that we should get rid of those things that are charming, or everything that does not have a practical value. In social life, gender *does* matter. The gestures in social life of men practicing small courtesies for women and vice versa should be retained.

Have you received any real howler letters?

If a letter's really ludicrous in itself, then someone probably made it up. Although I have overguessed on that, you know . . . I'll get one about a nude wedding or something like that and I think, "Oh, stop it." Then I get a couple of letters saying, "Oh no, I've been to one."

Now that you've been doing this column for twenty-five years, what issues do you think we need to pay attention to during the next twenty-five?

We've got a lot of unfinished business. Chiefly, to design a pattern of life that makes people able to attend to their duties—both their work and their private life, their friends and relatives, whatever responsibilities they have—without having to choose between them or shortchanging any of them.

What parting words would you give to our readers?

Behave yourself.

Patriotic Pride

by Ted Sorensen

Recapturing our idealism—and love of country—
one day at a time.

O n the Fourth of July, I am proud to be an American. In fact, I'm proud to be an American every day, including Halloween, Super Bowl Sunday and April Fools' Day. Patriotism is not the words one speaks or the flag one waves once or twice a year; it is the life one leads throughout the year, and I have been fortunate enough to lead a life filled with repeated opportunities to serve my country and fellow citizens.

Most of you have such opportunities. Not everyone, of course, has the chance to work in the White House or, like my daughter, to serve in the Peace Corps or, like my sons, to help, teach or counsel less fortunate children or, like my wife, to advance international understanding at the United Nations. But everyone who cares about this country can help to support it by paying his or her taxes, fulfill its principles by serving on a jury, help to assure its future by registering and voting for the ablest candidates and help to make it greater by contributing work or money to a local cause or charity. How blind are those who seek to evade any one of those obligations!

Most acts of patriotism in times of peace are not imposed as obligations. Rather, they arise when we least expect them, as a chance to make a difference: to tutor a disadvantaged student, for example, or campaign for an idealistic candidate; to volunteer for the neighborhood cleanup or take part in the town meeting. Nor is there any shortage of local and national organizations in this country that are truly doing good: helping to secure racial justice or world peace, distributing food to hungry children at home or to earthquake victims abroad, seeking action to curb pollution or expand after-school recreation. All you need is to "ask not what your country can do for you; ask what you can do for your country."

I remain convinced that this country, however flawed its past, however great its room for improvement in the future, is the one for me.

When John F. Kennedy spoke those words in 1961, I was particularly proud to be an American. It was not only his message that inspired me or the pageantry of peaceful change in national leadership (which, even if occasionally flawed, as we witnessed in Florida in November 2000, has been an American blessing as well as a necessity); it was my sense that our finest national values were at high tide. More than 60 percent of eligible voters—a level not equaled since—had cast their ballots in a presidential election that centered on issues, not personal attacks. Our in-boxes in the new administration were stuffed with job applications from America's brightest college graduates and young professionals, individuals who were more interested in Washington service than

Wall Street salaries. Old ideals and new ideas were in the air: exploring space, ending segregation, safeguarding our shores, expanding our economy, preserving our wilderness.

President Kennedy filled his cabinet (his so-called Ministry of Talent) with able and experienced leaders from both political parties, all of them men of commitment. (Alas, there were very few women in high government posts in those days.) Forsaking private-sector compensation, private life's leisures and, to a considerable extent, privacy itself, they were genuinely dedicated to fulfilling this nation's destiny as a "beacon . . . to the rest of the world," as the Founding Fathers had dreamed. Americans of widely differing backgrounds shared that spirit of dedication to the public interest.

Today the trends toward globalization in economics and regionalization in markets have somewhat diminished the importance of national flags. Every day enormous sums are electronically transmitted across national borders, with little regard for them. The impermeability of the nation-state's sovereignty under international law is less clear. The world is smaller; the American principles of free peoples and free markets are more universally applied; the notion of a global village is more real. National identity is less important to many.

But I am no less proud—or glad—to be an American. During these past forty years, my work has taken me to dozens of countries in every corner of the planet. Each has its outstanding attributes and assets. I truly learned something from every one of them. I could happily live in many of them, and I admire people in all of them. I am not interested in arguing questions of superiority, much less perfection, with any of them. But I remain convinced that this country, however flawed its past, however great its room for improvement in the future, is the one for me—the one whose basic principles, essential character and daily truths best meet my standards of heart and conscience. After I return from each first-time visit to another country, I am ever more grateful that this is my home.

I realize that many Americans have become grievously disillusioned or repeatedly disappointed during these past decades by Washington's role in Vietnam, Watergate and a parade of all-too-human flaws and failures. Many of them do not even vote, much less volunteer in an election campaign. Too many of them have lost their faith in democratic institutions and have turned cynical or apathetic about politics and public service. Too few of them seek civic responsibility or participation. Private employment offers more pay and less pain. Both the affluent and the underclass make their own material well-being their first priority.

But I talk with enough young lawyers and address enough young audiences and meet enough young friends of my daughter to know that the traditional American flames of civic virtue have not been quenched. "Of those to whom much is given, much is required." Contrary to an old shibboleth, the business of America is not just business. Nearly all our forebears came here, whether recently or long ago, for freedom and opportunity. To be a good American today is to help widen the horizons of freedom and opportunity for other Americans and, where we can, for peoples of other countries. To every citizen, I can say from experience: for at least part of your life, part of the time, give something back to this country. Put service ahead of self. Try it. You'll like it.

XI
THE MOTHER TONGUE

Protecting Our Language

by Anne H. Soukhanov

In the campaign to restore good grammar,
we must all carry the torch.

"To see him fumbling with our rich and delicate language is to experience all the horror of seeing a Sèvres vase in the hands of a chimpanzee," said Evelyn Waugh of Stephen Spender fifty years ago. Though Waugh's remark is one great English writer's criticism of another, it is apropos today if we change "him fumbling" to "them fumbling," because good English usage, as you may have noticed, is in a steep decline. As the editor of more than thirty dictionaries and other reference books, I have spent my professional career studying and recording the English language. These days I focus my time righting wrongs against our mother tongue. Unfortunately, there is a lot to keep me busy.

Remember when it was an event to find typographical errors in our newspapers or to hear bad grammar in newscasts? Now, if I don't encounter a howler a day, it's an event. Among some of my favorites from recent years:

• "The U.S. attorney better defeat me, because if they don't, they will be working in Yeehaw Junction." (Spoken by a U.S. congressman) *Failure to include the auxiliary verb* had *before better;*

lack of number agreement between the pronoun they *and its antecedent,* attorney.

• "Michael Jordan console's his mother." (Newspaper photo caption) *Insert of an incorrect apostrophe.*

• "State dinners . . . take two to three months to plan. Well, it's not like she didn't know what she was getting into." (Story in a major newspaper) *Faulty use of* like *as a conjunction.*

• "He lay his briefcase down on a chair and passed the darkened library. He turned on the light." (From a novel by an attorney-turned-author) *Past tense of the verb* to lay *is* laid, *not* lay.

• "They . . . should have just went along with the program." (Virginia high-school teacher) *Incorrect use of* went *(a form of the verb* to go) *where* have gone *is required.*

To protect the guilty, I have deliberately omitted the identities of the above abusers. However, slipups of this sort can be found in your local newspaper on a daily basis. Worse still are the errors made during television newscasts, which have a wider reach than the printed page. Among some of the language lapses we hear all too frequently: "It's time for Bernie and I to sign off." "The reason is because . . ." "The court opinion infers . . ." And "irregardless of the outcome . . ." When our so-called role models in the media make botcheries such as these, they creep into general usage.

In addition, we have witnessed a blurring of the distinction between formal and informal usage. For instance, when a newsmagazine introduces a story on drugs by calling them "way addictive," the distinction is blurred. Unsophisticated readers might wrongly assume that *way* is an acceptable substitute for *highly* in formal discourse.

Poor examples provided by pop musicians, athletes, politicians and the mass media, combined with apparent shortfalls in the American education system, have created a generation of young people who have not learned basic spelling and usage before leaving high school and encountering college freshman English.

For insight into the college generation's usage problems, consider the following examples of student writing submitted to the editors of the *Microsoft Encarta College Dictionary* by its advisory board of forty-one English professors: "Reading *Wuthering Heights,* Heathcliff never fails to make an impression." "Helen and me went to class." "This poem is'nt rhymed."

The number-one blunder cited by the professors in their students' writing is misuse of *there* as an invariably singular subject. President George W. Bush—a self-admitted English-language fumbler—had double trouble with *there* when he said, "I am willing to listen. There's a lot of opinions. There are a lot of opinions—there's a hundred opinions."

Apparently there are also a hundred opinions when it comes to vocabulary and spelling. The aforementioned professors offered examples such as *crucifiction* for *crucifixion, hoard* for *horde, anyways* for *anyway* and *pour* for *pore*. What's worse, when students mishear words, they create phrases like "by in large" for "by and large," "doggie dog" for "dog-eat-dog" and "note a republic" for "notary public."

America's undergraduates must realize that their mastery of written and spoken English will significantly influence their range of opportunities after graduation. Yet we cannot expect our children to speak well as long as all generations continue mispronouncing words. In the movies, in business and on the street, *relevant* often becomes *revelent; ask* is hacked into *ax*e; *et cetera* is transformed into "EK cetera"; and the biggest bomb of all, "NOO-kyuh-luhr" has mutated from "NOO-, or NYOO-, klee-uhr."

Even when there is no evident grammar problem, people tend to overwork certain words and expressions. "Charisma" lost its sparkle after being overused in the 1960s. In the 1980s, whether we were "credentialed" or "conflicted," we sought "empowerment" and "self-esteem." The 1990s brought a desire for "closure," in order to "deal with our issues," "move on with our lives" and vote for candidates with "gravitas." The twenty-first century is sure to bring its own set of trite phrases.

At times it seems that the battle to preserve the integrity of the English language is a losing one. Yet to win we must be willing to start on a small scale. Become your family's activist language mentor. Read to your very young ones. Encourage the older ones to read at levels higher than the norm. Buy your children dictionaries and show them that "looking it up" can be an adventure, whether on dictionary software or in print. Have spelling bees and award prizes. Encourage older children to handwrite drafts of their essays and to proofread their work before keying it. Explain that grammar- and spelling-correction software will not find and correct all mistakes. Software is a tool that assists, but does not think for, people.

If a child makes an error, gently point it out and explain the

> America's undergraduates must realize that their mastery of written and spoken English will significantly influence their range of opportunities after graduation.

correction. Check your children's school compositions before they submit them. Encourage youngsters to write graceful personal letters. Make a game of finding usage errors in print and on the air. Discuss them. Don't bow to the trends; take charge of your children's and grandchildren's language development.

Yet, as we all know, it is not just children who misuse English. So how do we handle the adult assaulters? The polite interlocutor will not, naturally, behave as a language-police officer. One can, however, repeat the original statement in conversational, paraphrased, corrected English, as if trying to verify what has just been said. Often the speaker, realizing something is amiss, will say, "Oh, sorry. What I meant to say was . . . " At the adult stage, however, bad habits are hard to break, so starting with our young ones appears to be our best hope for change.

"Language is the dress of thought," said the great English lexicographer Samuel Johnson more than two centuries ago. In this sense, we should always dress our language for success, not embarrassment and failure. Good English is an essential social grace, and it, like the Sèvres vase, ought not to be shattered.

Fighting Words

by Geoffrey Nunberg

How metaphors tinged with violence
have invaded our language.

The day major-league baseball teams resumed play after the September 11 attacks, I was watching the San Francisco Giants game on TV as the announcer Mike Krukow described the replay of a home run that Andres Galarraga had hit into the center-field bleachers. "Boy," Krukow said, "he really kil—he really hit that one good."

September 11 brought a lot of truths home to us, and one of them is that our ordinary language is saturated with metaphors of violence and destruction. (Actually, I first wrote "shot through with metaphors" and then thought better of it.) In the days and months after the attacks, the simplest conversation conjured up uncomfortable images, as if our inner screening devices had been ratcheted up to register the slightest suggestion of an ominous meaning. Last October, I was talking with a stockbroker about when the market might stage a recovery. "We'll see what happens when the dust clears," he said, then quickly added, "uh . . . so to speak." It's a tag you hear a lot these days, as people suddenly become sensitive to the literal definitions of their words.

Ordinarily, of course, those morbid meanings run so deep in the language that we don't register them at all. We don't hear any murderous undertones when someone talks about killing a baseball, not to mention killing a deal, the lights, an appropriations bill, the engine, a fifth of scotch, or a couple of hours between flights. And it seems natural enough to describe a woman as a femme fatale or as being drop-dead gorgeous. After all, the association between love and death is lodged deep in our collective psyche.

It does seem as if metaphors of death and mayhem have become more pervasive in recent years. A decade or so ago, mention of a "killer restaurant" would have brought images of ptomaine poisoning to mind; now it suggests a four-week wait for reservations. New companies and products used to fail; now they "crash and burn." When Internet start-ups began folding like houses of cards, we called them "dot-bombs."

> Over the last twenty years or so, America has made conversational mayhem a staple entertainment

Then, too, the tone of our language sounds a lot more bellicose than it used to. Carl von Clausewitz, the Prussian military theorist, is credited with saying that war is the continuation of politics by other means. But to listen to the way we talk in modern America, you might conclude the converse is true as well. Whatever we're talking about—politics, business, or sports—we tend to make it sound like an extension of warfare. It used to be that CEOs tried to model their language on that of business leaders such as Alfred P. Sloan, Jr., or Thomas

J. Watson, Sr.; now they're more likely to emulate George S. Patton or Captain Kirk. (Actually, the only topic that sounds less bellicose these days is warfare itself, which is increasingly described in language borrowed from business and sports: soldiers have become "assets," and killing someone has become a question of "taking him out.")

The Berkeley linguist George Lakoff has pointed out how easily we fall into martial metaphors when we're describing an argument or discussion: I shot down that proposal; her criticisms were right on target; you're liable to catch a lot of flak for that view; when she saw her position was indefensible, she abandoned it and took up a new line of attack.

You could say that this is all just a manner of speaking, and there's some truth to that. But it's no coincidence that people have taken to using belligerent metaphors at the same time that our public discourse has become a lot more uncivil and abrasive. Over the last twenty years or so, America has made conversational mayhem a staple entertainment, not just on *The Jerry Springer Show* but in the all-out rumbles that pass for political dialogue on TV. It sometimes feels as if the only way you can distinguish coverage of the Mideast turmoil from the panel discussions about it is to check which combatants are wearing neckties.

A critic might take all of this as a sign of the increasing violence and hardening of American culture. But this isn't the way that genuinely violent cultures talk. I'm willing to bet that speakers of Pashto don't slip so easily into murderous metaphors when they're talking about business or politics, not when the real thing is so painfully conspicuous in their lives. And I suspect that teenagers in Kandahar wouldn't be very susceptible to the appeal of styles of music with names like "dirge" and "death metal." (For that matter, I doubt whether the Afghans standing in line for food would see the charm of naming a dessert Death by Chocolate.)

On the contrary, the American penchant for using violent metaphors reveals the complacency of a people who have been able to pretend that death and conflict were kept at such a remove from their daily lives that they could get away with playing at them. If we can allow ourselves to be entertained by the invective of the political talk shows, it's because we expect that the guests are going to be chatting affably with one another as soon as the camera turns away rather than looking for a likely branch to throw a rope over.

By the same token, though the American marketplace may feel unforgiving, particularly in these tough times, it's hardly comparable to an honest-to-God battleground. Or for that matter, to the dog-eat-dog business world of Andrew Carnegie and John D. Rockefeller. These magnates would never have compared their activities to warfare. That would have hit too close to home in an age when strikers and scabs shed real blood and when there were no severance packages or unemployment benefits to keep laid-off workers from destitution or ruin. In 1906, when Upton Sinclair published his famous muckraking novel about the Chicago stockyards, he called it *The Jungle* to evoke images of relentless cruelty and violence. Nowadays people may still say "it's a jungle out there," but all they mean is that someone else is likely to pounce on your job or your client if you aren't careful.

In a sense, we shouldn't have needed September 11 to remind

us of how much self-delusion there was in the casual way we conjured up images of war, death and privation. After all, we always knew that it could happen here. American life has never been purged of its violence, and the safety net that seemed to permit us to talk about business as warfare has always been a little threadbare around the edges. The ironies were apparent for anyone who cared to look for them, but most of us didn't bother.

Granted, not even events as awful and far-reaching as those we endured in 2001 are likely to work a profound change in the way we talk. We'll get back soon enough to talking about murderous fastballs and shoes to die for—and why not? In California, some adolescents have already started to use *jihad* as a synonym for *cool*, probably by way of tweaking the ponderous solemnity that grown-ups bring to these topics.

But it will be a very long time before we emerge from the shadows cast by that day, and you hope that we'll have learned to be a little more circumspect in the meantime. From here on in, corporate executives will think twice before they accuse their competitors of practicing terrorist tactics, and people will be a little less quick to talk about a tragedy when the rain ruins a wedding supper. There's worse that can happen.

"Whatever" Do You Mean?

by Anne Taylor Fleming

With a single word, we can now dismiss one another
quickly and definitively.

I'm not exactly sure who first used it on me. It might have been my treasured teenage niece or one of my beloved step-granddaughters. Either way, I have the distinct memory that it was someone younger than I, someone to whom I was delivering a buoyant lecture about the importance of kindness or some such thing. The listener restlessly shifted her hips, rolled her eyes and departed with a one-word retort: "Whatever."

It was relatively light, that "whatever," a little singsongy, adolescent and good-natured. Nonetheless, I registered it hard. I had been dismissed, shut down, made to feel preachy and decidedly uncool. Could one little word be so powerful? It was an amazing lesson, a bracing one.

As the word has become the all-purpose, action-packed conversation-ender, many of us have "whatever" stories. Its use is not confined to kids. A friend of mine who is a professor vividly recalls the occasion when one of her esteemed colleagues used it during a faculty meeting. "Everyone was going around and around about something, the way academics do, and suddenly he said, 'Whatever.' It was a verbal existential shrug, as if to say,

'We're all wasting our time here. Does any of this really matter?' I was shocked. It made me sad, and it made me angry."

That's it. "Whatever" has become the word du jour for disengagement, a throwing in of the towel, an "excuse me, you're boring me, I can't listen to one more word you're saying, I'm outta here." If you're the recipient thereof, it's difficult to react. It seems so innocuous and yet so final at the same time, an impudent rebuke all dressed up in relative politesse. It can be delivered—and often is—with a smile, a wink or a lilt, which only adds to its trisyllabic tartness.

In a potty-mouthed, X-rated world, no single term is more maddening, more provocative, more symptomatic of the times—all this hip, cynical, slightly below-the-radar aggression packed into one lightweight word.

Let me back up for a minute. Poor old "whatever" has a benign and rather peaceable usage as well. It can be employed to connote true flexibility, as in: "What type of food would you like for dinner tonight?" Answer: "I don't know. Whatever." I have a new acquaintance who calls upon it a lot in this context as a way of signaling her amiability. "Whatever. You choose. I don't care. As long as we're together." Used that way, it does have an obliging sweetness.

An old friend of my husband's said the word every morning, on his knees, as a form of prayer. "Dear God . . . Whatever," meaning that he was prepared to accept whatever his Maker had in store for him. Each night he'd end the day, again on his knees, saying thank you.

But that's wholly different spiritual and verbal terrain. Mostly when people say "whatever" these days, it's in the new, mean, get-out-of-my-way way. To my ears, that evolution from the nice connotation of the word to the more malevolent one has happened roughly over the past decade.

"I hear people uttering it all the time," a smart, young twenty-something woman, one of my go-to people for cultural insight, tells me. "When they say 'whatever,' they're annoyed. They're hearing something they think is either stupid, a waste of their time or simply obvious. It is meant to communicate frustration."

And how does she respond when she hears it? "It hurts my feelings. I take it as a reprimand or a criticism. Given my personality, I'm likely to turn around and say, 'Whatever what? What's wrong with what I'm saying?' "

My oldest stepson, a successful writer and another of my cultural-insight resources, remembers saying it to a friend, who called him on it: "Oh, my God, you just 'whatever-ed' me."

According to my stepson, "This friend was really shocked because he thought we had the sort of relationship in which I would never 'whatever' him—that everything he had to say would be so interesting that I would never interrupt him or cut him off. I saw that he was right, and I apologized. It was a very insensitive thing to do."

As the story makes clear, to "whatever" a stranger is one thing; to "whatever" a friend is a much more serious slight. And, yes, it is a certifiable verb now. To "whatever" someone means to tell him, in short, to bug off (or the cruder, four-letter form).

So where did it come from? Why now? In part, because the word has become trendy—for adults as well as kids, make that for adults behaving like kids—a ready-made, socially acceptable insult for any and all occasions. But it goes deeper than that. My stepson is convinced that the rise of "whatever" is tied to the proliferation of technology.

"High-tech gadgets were supposed to give us more leisure time, but they've only given us more opportunity to cram stuff into our day," he says. "I believe the reign of 'whatever' can be tied to the rise of the cell phone. I'm on my mobile, I'm paying for these minutes and I don't have time to listen to your crap. So, 'whatever.' It's the multiuse term for the multitask generation, the verbal equivalent of the TV zapper. Zap, zap. I don't have time to listen to you anymore, so I'm just going to cut you off."

That resonates. In our techno-rich, caffeinated, workaholic culture, "whatever" is the pause button, the breather. Seen in that light, I have a whit more sympathy for the word, for its use, or at least, more sense of how it has overrun us. I relayed that theory to another younger cultural well-spring, and she agreed. But she pushes it even further. She says she thinks it has to do with information overload and a feeling of a lack of control—our inability to wade through all the daily blather that's coming at us from every which way and to try to discern any real truth in the mix, let alone to try to effect things. In short, we're back to the existential shrug.

To "whatever" someone means to tell him, in short, to bug off (or the cruder, four-letter form).

"I think the ascent of 'whatever' is symptomatic of a general powerlessness," she says. "You don't feel like you have a say; you can't get traction on anything. It's like the whole world is a sea of too much information, some of which may be true, while the rest isn't. You don't feel qualified to have a full-fledged opinion, but at the same time you're irked, so you respond with 'whatever.'"

That, too, seems smart—and certainly understandable from the vantage point of the younger generation. Everything is so hyped, so hurried, so intense. You want to opt out, cover your ears. You want to say "Shh!" to the world, even to those you love. You wonder, "How can I hear my own voice—take the measure of my own heart—when you're all talking at me all the time?" I get that now. I really get it, but that doesn't mean I am going over to the pro-"whatever" side.

The real message is that we—parents, bosses, all of us— have to slow down, draw a breath, hit the Pause button in a given day and listen to one another. No, not just listen, but hear, really hear, someone else, think about what's being said and what we, in turn, really think about it. That's the true task, and it will, no doubt, be a far harder one than simply deleting a word from our conversations.

XII
SEPTEMBER 11, 2001

Civility as Our
Greatest Defense

by David Brown

One of the many lessons we have learned in the wake of the horrific attacks on New York and Washington, D.C., is that in moments of crisis, our daily frustrations suddenly seem petty.

Although this sensation is certain to fade as time passes, perhaps we should recall this feeling the next time we order from a restaurant that has run out of the daily special or wait in a department-store line that seems to be going nowhere. Rather than lash out, we should use these occasions to step back and consider our real priorities. As we learned in September 2001, life is too short for rudeness.

—The Editors

O dd, isn't it, to think of that gentle word *civility* as something forceful? Yet the term has as many varied and contradictory verbal offspring as the canine species has breeds. What's so "civil" about civil war? Why does a "civil" action connote confrontation and discord? How about "civil" disobedience—what's civil about disobedience? Even the word *civilian* does not necessarily describe a peaceful person; it merely distinguishes one from a member of the armed forces.

I believe civility can be a defense against what makes life difficult and tiresome. An outstanding example is the calm and deeply compassionate behavior exhibited by the citizens of New York, Washington, D.C., and all of America, as well as that of other nations around the world after the horrific assault on our country. Following one of the greatest tragedies the United States has ever experienced, doctors, nurses, firefighters, police officers, construction workers, and others gave their all, and some of them, their lives, to assist the victims. There is perhaps no better example of how civility can rout inhumanity by disabling the offender with a show of grace and selflessness.

"Speak softly but carry a big stick," counseled President Theodore Roosevelt. When you counter boorish behavior in this way, it disarms the boor and the bore. In the case of the horrors of September 11, 2001, our "big stick" may be not a show of force but a show of civility.

This national tragedy has taught us that civility begins at home. A Chinese proverb holds that even husbands and wives should treat each other as guests. That means thanking each other on every occasion, including the act of love. My wife and I are meticulous in offering the same civility to each other as we do to courteous waiters and cab drivers.

As children, we were taught to say "thank you," "I'm sorry," and "pardon me." Civility is hereditary. Examples set by good parenting—how parents respond to each other—instruct children in the art of good manners.

In the grown-up world, I practice civility by thanking my secretary every night as she departs. The same treatment applies to cab drivers, even though they should be thanking me for my generous tips—and rarely do. The political establishment sets a poor example. "Because negative campaigning provides the biggest bang for the buck," writes commentator George F. Will, "it has become so incessant that good politicians are coarsened, and coarse people are drawn to politics."

My advice is this: a soft voice begets service. And gets results. An angry one begets an angry and uncertain response. The same rule applies to our dealings with government employees, department-store sales staff, and filling-station attendants. Even the worst of them will soften and melt when greeted by a friendly and understanding voice: "I know how terribly busy you are but . . . "; "When you can possibly find time, will you please . . . "; "The last thing you need is to go find this for me, but if you possibly could . . . "; and, of course, "Thank you" and "You're welcome." As the saying goes, honey attracts more flies than vinegar. But who wants flies? When we use common courtesy, we walk away with lower blood pressure and, often, our desired outcome.

Thank-you notes and gifts are obligatory after you have been invited to dinner at your host's home, to a restaurant, the theater or, most decidedly, to a country weekend. It's not enough to express gratitude on parting. A note and flowers must follow. Notes ought to be handwritten, not by the florist but by you. You know all that, of course, but it is the quality of the note and gift that makes your civility memorable. The note ought to memorialize something distinctive about the evening: a treasured wisp of conversation (preferably spoken by your host), the flowers, the guest list or the provenance of the wine.

Civility commands respect and affection. You may greet someone you do not know even on a city street. I have never been rebuffed when I smiled at comely ladies (of any age), who smile back or, just as often, smile first. In everyday life, civility extends to introductions. Never assume that everyone knows who you are, even if you are a celebrity. Believe it or not, former president General Dwight D. Eisenhower once announced to a stranger in an elevator, "I'm Dwight D. Eisenhower."

Whether you are the president of the United States or a vice president of sales, you must never forget to return telephone calls. This is an endemic problem in the entertainment industry. I could name names of those who never return a call. Indeed, I have an outstanding call to an agent that has not been returned in seventeen years. There are other examples too insufferable to mention. The noncallers are bums, boobs and barbarians.

> Civility commands respect and affection.

I would like to note, however, that there is a point beyond which civility becomes unctuous and patently insincere. Canada has prided itself on being perhaps the world's most polite country. I made a comedic point of this in a scene from a sparsely attended (except in Canada) film titled *Canadian Bacon,* in which a gang of American ruffians rides roughshod over startled Canadians, who whimper responses such as "I'm sorry" or "excuse me." Although this is an extreme example, there is no point in thanking overtly hostile or bombastic individuals. In cases such as these, walking away is the best weapon civility has to offer. Silence is also appropriate. Never descend to the level of the offender. That can only gratify him or her. Stooping to the barbaric levels of our transgressors is not the answer. Regardless of the situation, in the end, civility always carries the day.

What's Really Important

Interviews by Francine Maroukian

A collection of insights

After the tragic days of autumn 2001, *Town & Country* surveyed some of its friends—writers, designers and other tastemakers—about life's true necessities.

Karim Rashid, industrial designer: What really endures are artifacts, effigies, things that speak about a time, place or civilization. When people say to me that everything seems trivial or meaningless, I believe the opposite. Objects outlive us, and they are the symbols of our culture and history. Every object in one's life should bring heightened meaning, pleasure or function, or there is no need for it.

Mireille Guiliano, President and CEO, Clicquot, Inc.: I have never been a "material" girl. Now more than ever, what matters most to me are family, friends, taking some time for myself and doing good for others. Certainly laughter, sharing, charity and conviviality are key values that have been reaffirmed. I am fortunate in my personal and professional life to have the opportunity to travel and to learn about other cultures, to share a good meal with interesting people—and to listen.

Alain de Botton, writer: We are living in a land not unlike the Roman Empire in the first century A.D. The Roman empire, comparable to the "American empire," was almighty, and yet it kept being shaken by various events. There were political disturbances (the reigns of Caligula and Nero); terrorism (from the barbarian hordes hiding in the German forests); and natural disasters (the destruction of Pompeii and earthquakes in Italy). Wise people of the time found solace in a philosophy of life called Stoicism. This doctrine advised people to place value only in those things that could not be destroyed, that were beyond the reach of fortune. These things were, in essence, anything that you can do in your own mind without the need of anyone else. This belief did not, however, imply solipsism. You can think of other people, and indeed love them in your own mind, even if they have been killed. The point is to learn to be content with your own thoughts and feelings rather than trying to control and tame the whole world. There is a lot of wisdom there, I think.

Oscar de la Renta, designer: What endures are family and friendships—and the knowledge that every day, somewhere, there is a beautiful sunrise.

John Loring, design director, Tiffany & Co.: Real values are constant, and what matters now is what mattered before. There are things that happen in the world that can serve to make you more aware of values. But the values don't change. What continues to be valuable in life is love, compassion, generosity of spirit, respect for others and ourselves and continual gratitude. Some people ask, "What should I do now?" Do your best. This is not a moment to slow down; this is the time to accelerate in the pursuit of everything positive and excellent in all aspects of life—your relationships, your work, whatever it is that makes your life better.

Diana Krall, artist: I'm always thankful for the good

relationships I have with my family and friends; that's what keeps me standing strong. But what has become more important is that we come out of our self-protective bubbles, that we look people right in the eye and ask "How are you?"; that we acknowledge our collective experience rather than live in our own little worlds.

François Nars, photographer, president and creative director, NARS Cosmetics, Inc.: An incident of this magnitude deepens your love of family, reinforces your values and reminds you how important they are; we need to hold on to them! I've realized that freedom is a gift; we have to fight to keep it.

Amanda Foreman, author of *Georgiana, Duchess of Devonshire*: I think we all know in our hearts what really matters. Occasionally our lives become so busy that we partly forget, but our core values will always remain our core values. However, since September 2001, I have recommitted myself to bringing history into the present. I believe that we, as individuals, connect with humanity through the stories of our ancestors. The journey of history is the passage of the mind from ignorance to enlightenment. History will not tell us what to do, but it will show us who we are.

Carolina Herrera, designer: Family and friends are what I value the most. Faith, hope, love, friendship and caring for others are what last and mean the most in life.

Judith Krantz, novelist: What endures: a sense of humor; the will to retain optimism, fortitude and tenacity; celebrations, no matter how small; the vital importance of seeing your friends more often rather than less often; continuing to work for causes that concern more than your personal well-being; reading— keeping a good book on your night table and finding time to read it; growing green plants in your home; nature—if you can spend time outdoors, in a park or in the country, stay as long as possible; the need to keep in touch with every friend you've ever made, by snail mail, e-mail or, best of all, telephone; eating and exercising intelligently; and enjoyment, wherever you find it. What seems unimportant: envy of the insides of other people's houses or closets; status symbols; being cool, trendy or cutting-edge; holding on to old grudges; regrets about past decisions.

Daniel Boulud, chef and owner, Daniel: For me what endures is cooking, and not just because it is my passion and my focus, but because it brings people together in a way that offers comfort and even joy.

Countess Simonetta Brandolini d'Adda, owner, The Best in Italy, villas: In this difficult time, one looks to family and friends around the world, caring in an acute way that we remain safe in a world without pain. Trust in God, our health and our freedom remain core values as well as deeply felt caring for the world's artistic masterpieces, that they may be spared damage or destruction, as they are our signposts for the future.

> What endures are family and friendships—and the knowledge that every day, somewhere, there is a beautiful sunrise.

Stanley Marcus, Chairman Emeritus, Neiman Marcus: It seems to me that what matters now is the same as what mattered on September 11 or July 4 or February 14.

James de Givenchy, jewelry designer, Taffin: What matters is creation at every level. We spend a short time on earth, and it is incredible to make something of beauty that moves someone. Whether it be music, art, or life . . . it's what makes us human.

Laura Mercier, makeup artist and cofounder, Laura Mercier Cosmetics: I think this is the time to pursue happiness, no matter where you find it: with friends and family, in relationships or in the passion you may have for the work you do.

Leonard Lauder, Chairman, Estée Lauder Companies: Since what I value is the spirit that drives New York, I think the most important responsibility we have is to rebuild the city.

> Being with family and friends, whether at home or abroad, is what matters.

Geoffrey Kent, Chairman and CEO, Abercombie & Kent Group: What matters to me most intimately is my immediate family, the A&K family, my friends and the natural world. On a more universal scale, what matters to me is the freedom to travel, which I believe is the key to our humanity; when a culture has contact with another culture, there is a connection, and that is the only thing that can bridge the gaps in our understanding of one another.

Barbara Barry, designer: Throughout this time of introspection, I have wanted to be at home. My home and my surroundings have become my place of healing. I have questioned all that I do and whether it has value. I believe it does, as I see my work in terms of how it serves to create an environment for people to find more meaning in their lives. It is not about design but about what design can do for us by supporting us and creating a safe haven in a hectic world.

George Butterfield, Founder and President, Butterfield & Robinson Travel: Being with family and friends, whether at home or abroad, is what matters. We have just witnessed one of the most horrific acts in history. People's lives and relationships have been shattered. Everyone is reevaluating the importance of relationships and spending more time nurturing them. Only memories really endure. People will want greater and greater experiences to add to the memory book of life.

Antonia Bellanca, perfumer, Antonia's Flowers: What to do and how to live now? The same as always, and in fact I feel confident that I have had my priorities straight. It's so simple in many respects: live each day as if it's your last; do everything reasonable that Hallmark cards implore you to do: smell the flowers, tell your family and friends how much you love them as many ways and times as possible each day; do not work long hours in order to buy things for your family that will ultimately be your family's undoing by taking you away from one another. And teach your children well.

Cathy Waterman, fine jeweler: I've always awakened with a deep sense of gratitude for my family and my friends, for the sunlight through the leaves as I'm out for an early-morning walk and for the "good morning" from a neighbor along the way. Now I'm equally grateful for the courage of ordinary men and women who do extraordinary things, for my fellow citizens who are joined together in an experiment in democracy that worships freedom and for the spiritual values that nourish us all.

Wynton Marsalis, Artistic Director, Jazz at Lincoln Center: The thing that must endure is the will to come together and celebrate.

What I've Learned

by Peggy Noonan

In the years since the attacks on America, we're still
discovering who we are and who we want to be.

T he impulse of tragedy is on to life and more
life," said Eugene O'Neill, who pondered the
power of sadness to shape a life and to edify.
I used to think of the quote sometimes when
I attended a funeral: this sad thing we're
doing makes me feel more tender toward the
sidewalk I will soon walk home on, and toward the home itself.

Sometimes I think of a wonderful man named Nicky
Forstmann, who died too soon, in his fifties, a few years ago. I
didn't know him well, only liked him from afar. He once asked
me to his home to discuss a book he had written about what he'd
learned from life. He was so sick but full of a kind of sweetness
and enjoyment, and I told him what I thought: his book had big
and powerful things in it, and, yes, he should publish it. He, his
elegant wife and I had a happy lunch afterward in a little dining
area lined by windows that overlooked Central Park. It was so
beautiful. We had white wine and lively conversation—no one
was shy or hidden—and we kind of discovered one another. He
laughed out loud at one point and said, "You are beautiful!" He
spoke with such discovery, such relish, that we both laughed. He

meant: I'm dying, and I see your humanity and it touches my heart. His wife teased him—"He says that to everyone now," she said—and I thought, "Of course he does. He's dying, and he sees how wonderful we all are."

So these things, the O'Neill quote and the Forstmann memory, are expressions of how September 11 affected me. It didn't change me; it reinforced me or, rather, reinforced the me I'd been becoming.

It made me hungrier for life and more grateful for it. I feel more actively grateful. My gratitude is more present as I walk down the street and see small things: how an infant who doesn't know how to kiss yet, kisses her mother by putting her whole face up against her mother's; the skinny, tender arms of eight-year-old boys; the light on Montague Street in Brooklyn in the summer when the sun starts to go down and hits the great skyscrapers across the river and fills Brooklyn Heights with a gold-dust glow.

You know who expressed this beautifully without saying it? My fourteen-year-old son, who was trapped in Brooklyn at school and unable to make it back to our home in Manhattan that terrible day. He was near the Brooklyn Promenade; he watched the sun set on the river as he looked at the exploded city; he saw the amazing density of the cloud that marked the amazing loss. And a stunning thing happened: when dusk came, the falling sun hit the buildings, lit the smoke, and the million pieces of paper still swirling in the air. For an instant it all looked like sparkling confetti, brilliant fireworks, whirling gold, pink and gray, and he got through to me on the phone and said, "Mom, it was so beautiful," and his voice had wonder in it. Wonder and horror that such destruction could, for a moment, be transmuted into such glory. Of all the things I will never forget from that day, the first is the wonder in his voice.

I'll never forget any of it. None of us will. One columnist speculated that 20 million people saw it from nearby with their own eyes, saw the attack or the fire or the fall or the wounding gorgeousness of the cloud, which lingered for days afterward. I live here and I was one of them. For months after September 11, I would think of the clusters of Vietnamese women who suddenly, after the Vietnam War, began to go blind. Doctors said it was hysterical blindness, visual overload: the trauma they'd seen had left them unable to see, at least for a time. I keep wondering: will some of the millions develop a case of hysterical blindness? And what is it we will not be able to see?

Meanwhile, I feel I have more clarity. I see better. I am more grateful to be alive. I take greater joy in smaller things, but here is the big thing: I feel more certain than ever that there is a God, that he is good, that there is purpose and meaning in the world, in my life, in yours. I thought tragedy was supposed to shake your faith. Mine has only deepened, and this is true of almost everyone I know. On the nine-month anniversary of the attacks, a friend sent me a note that said what I had been driving at in my work and my thoughts but not quite saying or reaching. She was recalling a quote from C. S. Lewis. She couldn't remember the words, but the meaning was this: Institutions come and go, but the waiter who poured your coffee this morning is eternal.

Meaning, the things of the world, the things we create, do not last forever but a soul does. A human soul lives forever in eternity. Great buildings rise and fall, but souls continue onward, and you affect a soul for well or ill every time you interact with a human being.

This is a big thought, and a reordering one. It reminds us of our profound and enormous power every day as we talk to, love, shame or ignore each other. That's the big drama—the human person.

I feel more certain than ever that, for whatever reason or reasons, we, those of us who live now in America, have been put here to get our country through the big terrible thing and the things that will follow. That is our job. I have a purpose and so do you. It is: Get through, hold fast, move forward, hold together, make the future. And do it with brio, with heart.

I think we all somehow know this without any of us saying it. Which is why since September 11 so many of us are more generous with those we know and don't know, more delicate, more patient, more polite. We are

I feel I have more clarity. I see better. I am more grateful to be alive. I take greater joy in smaller things.

better to each other on the subway, smile more, connect more on the street. We're more welcoming to strangers. Because we're all in it together, and we know it. And we've been reminded that life is precious and full of beauty. We are more hungry for it than ever, and so hurtle toward it and through it with more courage and love.

GOING QUIETLY

XIII
CAN YOU HEAR ME NOW?

Celling Out
by Thomas P. Farley

Mobile phones in hand, we are now in touch twenty-four/seven. Except, that is, with our manners.

Twenty years ago, our movie screens were glowing with the story of an extraterrestrial who desperately needed to "phone home." What made this implausible tale so appealing in 1982 was that we all could identify with being in a remote location without a way to contact loved ones. These days, that concept sounds hopelessly primitive. A sophisticated traveler like E.T. would surely have a sleek flip phone and a calling plan with no roaming charges. With one touch of the speed dial, he could sit back, enjoy a few Reese's Pieces and be home before dinner.

Ironically, it's we earthlings who have started to resemble aliens. Our cities are now filled with people who walk with their elbows in the air and mini-antennae protruding from their ears. Still others stride on sidewalks, hands at their sides, talking (it seems) to no one but themselves.

Phone-aholics just can't seem to resist the hurdy-gurdy sounds these devices make. No matter what they are doing, these addicts will drop everything to take an incoming call. It matters not that they are on a dinner date or in a business meeting. "Is that me?" they ask as they earnestly dive into their bags in search of the wailing offender. Woe to the would-be talker who discovers dejectedly that the ringing phone is someone else's.

Although such scenes are now ubiquitous, it was not long ago when the only people able to afford mobile phones kept them in a mahogany box in the back of their limousines. Even when these handy gadgets reached the masses, airtime was so costly that users kept their discussions short and sweet.

In this century, of course, talk is cheap. Enticed by calling plans that offer "free nights and weekends" or 4,000 "anytime" minutes, many of us are obsessed with chatter. Beaming through the airwaves as you read this are such lines as "I'm at the market . . . should I buy seven-grain or wheat?" and "Would you believe it? Some kid just kicked sand on my blanket!"

No matter where we are, whether the bread aisle or the beach, when our overstimulated attention spans wear thin, the cell phone provides a diversion. Perish the thought that we might take time to hear ourselves think. And with so many people talking, you have to wonder who's doing the listening.

According to the Cellular Telecommunications & Internet Association in Washington, D.C., forty-five percent of the U.S. population have cell phones. Where does that leave the remaining fifty-five? They are most likely in a movie, on a treadmill or at a restaurant not far from a thoughtless gabber who is acting as if he were holed up in a private phone booth. As a result, it's not just the phone owners who are doing the talking. Bring up the topic of cell-phone abuse at a cocktail party, and you're likely to get an earful of horror stories: the "Ode to Joy" during church services that emanates not from an organ but from a neglected phone. Women queuing up outside the ladies' room while one of their own chats away in a much-needed stall. Cashiers who roll their eyes when they have to stop midconversation to answer a customer's query. Cab drivers who career in and out of traffic while conversing cellularly. Business travelers who hide beneath their tray tables to get in one last sales pitch before takeoff. We've even lost the simple pleasure of being in a restaurant without the *William Tell Overture* and the *Flight of the Bumblebee* battling in the air.

On the rare occasions when their phones are not playing these classical tunes, airtime gluttons will testify "I don't know how I *ever* managed without my phone." Yet, for the majority of the 126 years since Bell first called Watson, we did manage without phones on our hips. How did we get by? When we needed to talk with someone by phone, we would simply wait until we got home. No longer. "Nowadays when I take my kids to the park," says a suburban mother of two, "all of the moms stand around talking on their phones. Yet we never speak with one another."

If the marathon talkers were more considerate, it might not be so bad. Unfortunately, we must endure their bellowing: "What's that? You're breaking up. Hey, John, stay right there. I'm going to call you back." And cellular service being what it is, poor John is lucky if he can decipher every other word.

Even the call of the wild cannot drown out the call of the StarTAC. Many bikers, in-line skaters and joggers have long since decided that the best way to pass the time while exercising is to multitask. After all, why just pedal when you can trade stocks at the same time? And chances are, your broker is executing the transaction from an airport lounge, a car pool, a bus or a train.

Yes, thanks to cell phones, we are more connected today than ever. Yet that very same connectedness has brought its share of disconnection, too. And I'm not talking about dropped signals. Many of us are simply abandoning in-person communication. In the process, we're losing a degree of empathy that can be expressed only through body language and eye contact.

Fortunately, there are some who have realized that our urge to talk—regardless of time or place—has gone too far. President Bush has been known to cast an evil glare at reporters whose cell phones go off during his press conferences. Depending on his mood, he'll also stop his remarks midsentence and recite his speech over from the beginning. In San Diego, the cellular nuisance became so bothersome that the mayor held a Cell Phone Courtesy Week, encouraging users to "mind their mobile manners." Many restaurants, schools, theaters and golf clubs tell their patrons the same thing. And on Amtrak's northeast corridor trains, if you make a beeline for a Quiet Car, the only high-pitched tone you'll hear aboard is the conductor's whistle.

> If you own a phone, remember to turn it off before entering a house of worship, a theater or a library.

Yet even the most ardent cell-phone haters would agree that mobile technology now plays a vital role in our lives. On September 11, it enabled many ill-fated office workers and air travelers to say their final good-byes to family and friends. For countless other people—from stranded hikers to heart-attack victims—having a portable link to the outside world has been a literal lifesaver. Thus, the benefits of cell phones certainly outweigh the aggravations.

The lesson for us all, however, is that modern convenience must not tempt us to forgo common consideration. If you own a phone, remember to turn it off before entering a house of worship, a theater or a library. Always keep your phone off the dinner table and keep your ring setting simple, or better yet, use its vibrate feature instead. And if you have a poor connection, don't expect the party on the other end to decrypt your staccato utterings; try the call again from a landline.

If there is only one message to rise above the cellular din, let it be this: if you can't avoid conversing in a public place, keep your discussion short, to the point and quiet. The phone company may not thank you, but those of us around you surely will.

The Art of Listening
by Letitia Baldrige

Are we getting so good at having our say that
we're forgetting to let others have theirs?

I n case you don't think anyone is actually listening to
you—or to anyone else, for that matter—you're not
alone. Listening has become a lost art. Whereas children were once brought up to understand the importance of paying attention to the person speaking,
today's child grows into adulthood all too adept at
thrusting his own conversational agenda upon others, carefully
guarding the license to interrupt at will.

Not that kids are the only culprits. The major complaint I
hear among the senior executives I encounter in my corporate
etiquette consulting is that their managers don't listen to them.
And here in Washington, D.C., where I live, the political pundits
are past masters of interrupting, of making their various points
despite any relevance they may have to the topic at hand. How
can adults expect young people to listen when we've gotten so lax
about it ourselves?

No doubt we could make more time for listening if we
weren't devoting so much attention to our technology. The family
raconteur may simply be no match for the razzle-dazzle of the
newest computer game or the latest offering on the Internet. Our

increasingly frenetic schedules also seem to discourage listening of any quality: it's as if parents and children, or husbands and wives, would never have the time to discuss the things they need to if they allowed themselves—and each other—the luxury of full sentences without disruption.

Back in the 1950s, during my days at the American embassy in Rome, I learned an important lesson about listening from a most dashing teacher, the Italian film director Roberto Rossellini. The two of us shared the same garage on the Viale Bruno Buozzi, and we often exchanged pleasantries. One night after parking our cars (his a sleek, custom-made Ferrari; mine a stubby little Morris Oxford), he asked me if I was enjoying my life in Italy. Very much, I told him, and then he offered this advice: *"Ascoltami bene, Letizia"* (Listen well, Letitia), "because you cannot understand Rome without listening to her; the distinctive noises of her streets, the cars, Vespas, people arguing, singing—they're all synchronized to the beat of her heart." I told him that I would always listen to the beat of Rome's heart, but I also wanted to add, "It's very easy to listen to the sounds of this place when people like you are doing the talking."

> Good listeners know how to draw out other people, making them look good by asking questions that match their expertise.

If you've spent over four decades toiling in some pretty fancy vineyards, you should be able to pick up a few good tips on the art of listening. I have noticed after years of diplomatic and White House service as well as a long business career, that there are certain common characteristics in good listeners:

- They don't interrupt—ever—unless the house is on fire.
- They aren't afflicted with wandering pupils. When someone is talking to them, they look him or her straight in the eye. If you keep looking for someone more famous or exciting to talk to, you'll be a dead duck socially.
- Good listeners know how to draw out other people, making them look good by asking questions that match their expertise.
- They learn while they listen. That's the whole point of it: dismiss the trivial and file away the substantive.

Among the more adroit practitioners of skilled listening I've ever observed was the Duchess of Windsor. She always knew just how to flatter any man of rank and importance within her range—and her range was pretty awesome. When she was invited to a party, she always had the guest list read to her ahead of time (a very rude request for us mere mortals), so she knew exactly who would be sitting to her left and right and, therefore, which other VIPs she should seek out during cocktails and the coffee hour. "Mr. Secretary," she would say, patting a satin cushion beside her, always on the prettiest settee in sight, "do come sit here. I am longing to talk to you." (There was no room, of course, for anyone else to sit with them.) She would ask him a couple of very important questions and then spend the rest of her time listening, agreeing amiably with his points, and throwing in a comment or two when it seemed necessary. If she were chatting with the secretary of agriculture, he would have thought she owned five thousand acres of Nebraska farmland and studied the temperament of the grain market.

In her White House days, Jacqueline Kennedy Onassis was famous for the way she would listen to the high-ranking man beside her. She'd fix her gaze on the totally mesmerized fellow and, after a while, utter something witty or astute to him, her voice softened to a whisper. Invariably, her dinner partner would lean in even closer and give the appearance of whispering something back in supreme confidentiality. It was supremely sexy, too. (I once asked Jackie what she had been saying to the Italian ambassador at dinner the night before. He had looked bewitched. With a straight face, her signature wit in fine form, Jackie replied, "We were evaluating Washington's private schools for our children, Tish." I never asked her that kind of question again.)

One thing Jackie would *never* do is talk too much. Would that we all could be so considerate. There are some signs, though, that it's time to stop talking and start listening. It's that time when:

- Your listener's eyes begin to glaze over. There is a lot of body shifting, such as legs crossing and uncrossing and people slumping in their chairs.
- Too many people are refilling too many water glasses.
- You see people yawning and trying to catch their yawns in midflight.
- A person's comeback is a total non sequitur.
- You notice your abductee's eyes darting around the room, desperately seeking any pair of eyes except yours.

I remember discussing the sorry state of listening over lunch with the ever-delightful hostess Alyne (Mrs. Jack) Massey of Nashville. She agreed that it's important to "act completely interested in the person who's speaking, even if you're not." When someone at the table objected, saying, "That's just being hypocritical," Alyne countered, "I don't think making someone glad to be sitting next to you is hypocrisy. It's just being kind."

What I Should Have Said

by Philip Herrera

There's no better way to defuse uncomfortable
social situations than with deft rejoinders.
Alas, they often occur to us a little too late.

We all know that Mark Twain, when he learned that some newspapers had published accounts of his death, dryly noted that the reports were "an exaggeration." And that Samuel Johnson, in the midst of some friendly banter about travel in the British Isles, remarked, "The noblest prospect which a Scotchman ever sees is the high road that leads him to England." And that James McNeill Whistler, when Oscar Wilde exclaimed "I wish I'd said that," in appreciation of one of Whistler's quips, murmured, "You will, Oscar, you will."

These are splendid ripostes. They spring hot and fresh from the brain and are memorable for being apt and perfectly timed. If only the rest of us could think so well and so fast! But the sad truth is most people don't think up witty retorts on the spot. Much more often, they come to mind after the fact. The French call this phenomenon *l'esprit de l'escalier*—the repartee that occurs to us on the staircase as we leave the party.

If it occurs to us at all. I know a musician in New York who suddenly realized he needed to relieve himself while he was still quite far from his apartment. Spotting a restaurant he frequented, he dashed inside and noticed a sign that read "Restrooms for the use of our customers only." He anxiously asked if he could use the bathroom, but the owner simply replied, "Can't you read the sign?" "That statement made me so mad that I've thought a lot about what I should have answered," the musician says. "I'm still looking for something both pointed and elegant." But he has come up empty so far, and one has to wonder how sweet his revenge would be at this stage, anyway. Wit, when stored away in the mind, has a marked tendency to turn insipid, like food on a steam table.

But retorts sometimes have a way of bubbling up to the surface, even if belatedly. A pretty blonde (who, like everybody interviewed for this piece, asked to remain anonymous) tells of a formal party in Philadelphia: "I got all dressed up, and one of my husband's friends greeted me by saying that I looked terrific. Then he said he'd like to see me naked. I choked out something like 'Fat chance!' but minutes later, I knew what I should have said: 'Blondes prefer gentlemen.'"

Indeed, nothing seems to inspire people to wish for a second shot at a comeback more than a perceived insult. But wit should be the response of choice. It is much more satisfying than anger on all counts. Laughter neatly defuses situations that could easily become testy and still allows the speaker to feel the glow of minor triumph. Wit isn't itself rude, though it can come gratifyingly close.

Just this past Easter, a lady of a certain age was greeted by an old beau who told her that she was "looking good—I can see vestiges of your former beauty." At the time, she was flabbergasted. By now, she has formulated her retort: "But can I see vestiges of *your* former charm?" A New Yorker reports a similar incident: "I met an acquaintance who said, 'Oh, Margaret, you look so fresh and nice. Have you had a face-lift?' I replied as coolly as I could, 'No, I haven't.' But I should have said, 'Do you really believe that blunder is the sincerest form of flattery?'" Such responses have the nice, crisp resonance of a slap.

Besides, if we give in to anger, the right phrase is almost certain to come to us too late. A Boston Brahmin, when told by a fellow club member that he was getting fat, absorbed the remark in outraged silence. His mind had turned to fudge, and no zinger occurred to him. But sometime later, he heard an aphorism and adopted it as he replayed the scenario in his head: "A waist is a terrible thing to mind."

> Nothing seems to inspire people to wish for a second shot at a comeback more than a perceived insult.

A young broker in the Hamptons was distraught when his wife, in her eighth month of pregnancy, came home weeping. It turns out that a man in a store had looked her over and said, loudly enough that she could hear, "Huge." Shocked, her husband told her, "You shouldn't pay attention to such a rude man." A more clever response, he has since decided, was "He wasn't looking at your stomach, honey. He was looking at your engagement ring."

There are times when a comeback benefits from being

belated; the extra beat enhances the humor. German artist Kurt Schwitters is said to have traveled to Vienna to meet the great expressionist painter Oskar Kokoschka. He climbed the stairs to Kokoschka's studio and knocked timidly on the door. Kokoschka opened it, heard the visitor stammer his admiration, and abruptly announced, "I am not Kokoschka!" "Oh," Schwitters said, and he started walking down the stairs. A few steps down, he turned and said, "And I'm not Schwitters."

But that's an exception to the rule for repartee, which emphasizes spontaneity. A woman executive I know, a former model, usually wears a pantsuit when she travels. Going through airport security recently, she was told by the agent: Take off your shoes and open your pants. She complied, then thought of what she should have said: "Aren't we at least going to have dinner first?"

What happens to these unspoken bons mots? Most, alas, are lost. It's difficult for us to create a scene today into which yesterday's rejoinder will fit snugly. Some people try anyway. One elderly member of a prominent New York family apparently used to spend afternoons in her bath, plotting whole dialogues that would allow her to deliver the verbal felicities she had confected. "At dinner, she would wrench the conversation around," recalls her granddaughter, "but almost never was she able to use one of her quips." We all share her feelings of disappointment. In the world of wit, there are precious few second chances.

The Proliferation
of Pretension

by Joe Queenan

Ralph Waldo Emerson once said, "The mark of
the man of the world is absence of pretension."
Oh, if Emerson could only see us now.

Many years ago I fled New York City for its tony northern suburbs. Some friends actually believed that I relocated to Westchester County because I wanted to put down roots, but the truth is I left New York to get away from pretentious people. By the time the moving van arrived, I'd had it up to here with friends prattling on about Rainer Werner Fassbinder, Umberto Eco and the Kronos Quartet or rhapsodizing about the director's cut of Satyajit Ray's *Pather Panchali.*

The thing I liked about the suburbs—other than the panoramic vistas and short lines at the post office—was that pretentious people generally felt out of place there. Over the years, the suburbs had consistently failed to address the needs of the constitutionally pretentious, refusing to erect the infrastructure of intellectual ostentation that makes Manhattan, Boston and San Francisco such hotbeds of hot air. Lacking avant-garde theaters, Frank Gehry museums and swanky art-house cinemas, pretentious people living outside the major metropoli were forced to drive into the city in order to satisfy their craving for clever *aperçus* and witty repartee.

Though museums do exist in *campagna,* they have never been able to marshal the resources to mount anything resembling the Whitney's massive 2000 exhibition of Barbara Kruger's ironic, prefab banalities. This was the sort of show that affords the cognoscenti a chance to trade thoughts on postmodern semiotics, feminist deconstructionism and subversive neo-Marxist graphic design while on their lunch breaks from Morgan Stanley. Sadly, in the suburbs, such opportunities rarely presented themselves. So locals had to stick with traditional favorites: reminiscing about the good old days at Exeter, correcting the maid's pronunciation of "cabernet," bragging about having never seen *Who Wants to Be a Millionaire* and pretending not to know who Eminem is.

By the time my first child was born, I honestly felt that I had outgrown pretentiousness, which seemed like an undergraduate affectation.

It is not that the suburbs lack pretentious inhabitants; my own circle of friends includes several who would gladly ford raging torrents for the chance to stare at a grainy print of a sixty-five-year-old Marcel Carné film (provided it was the *version originale*). The problem for these people has never been the will to be pretentious; it has always been a question of venue.

I do not mean to suggest that I myself am incapable of cultural name-dropping or the cunningly rehearsed *bon mot.* A lifelong Francophile, I am as comfortable discussing thematic inconsistencies in the work of Abbé Prévost as I am chatting about the influence of Valenciennes on Théodore—though not Le Douanier—Rousseau. But by the time my first child was born, I honestly felt that I had outgrown pretentiousness, which seemed like an undergraduate affectation. Besides, while my children were small, I was so burdened by the responsibilities of fatherhood that I did not have time to be pretentious. I was too busy watching films like *Curly Sue*.

For many years I enjoyed my sojourn in the provinces. But not so long ago I noticed that things were changing. People I was accustomed to chatting with exclusively about ice hockey and school taxes suddenly began alluding to enigmatic productions of *Pelléas et Mélisande* and concerts paying homage to Astor Piazzolla. Oh, no! Pretentiousness was coming to my neighborhood.

It started quietly, with the Hudson Valley Writers' Center, which offered such classes as "Tapping Creativity: Dreams, Mandalas and Shaping Images into Writing," not to mention "Writing as Healing." Sadly, this was but the first manifestation of an intellectual efflorescence that would soon engulf the county, a cultural Blitzkrieg that would send low-brows into hiding, leaving nothing prosaic in its wake. In short order came the dainty tea shops with *I Puritani* playing in the background, and the poetry readings by the local baristas, leveling hoi polloi with a fusillade of pith. And then, inevitably, the bookstore clerks who acted as if anyone buying a John Grisham novel—while Eco went ignored—should be deported.

Molto, molto raffinato.

Much as I was disconcerted by the rising tide of snootiness,

I still felt that there was something piecemeal, unfocused, and therefore harmless about this onslaught. The vortex lacked an epicenter; my beloved county did not yet boast a single institution poised to sate the ravenous appetites of the pretentious on a daily basis.

Then, in 2001, the Jacob Burns Film Center arrived.

Yes, the tipping point was the opening of an art-house cinema, the one-stop shopping center for the self-important. For decades, the dinky Fine Arts Cinema in Scarsdale was the only theater in all of Westchester where it was possible to see a riveting three-hour movie about the making of *The Mikado* and then have a lofty tête-à-tête afterward. But the Fine Arts had only one screen and a Lilliputian lobby, forcing patrons to huddle outside in the freezing cold, waiting to see the movie in which Holly Hunter gets dragged overboard by a grand piano attached to her ankle.

Now risking pneumonia is no longer required. Incongruously positioned in Pleasantville's nondescript "downtown," the Burns center is an upscale, no-riffraff arts complex that not only shows nightly screenings of Belgo-Bosnian black comedies but also hosts gatherings at which audience members are encouraged to air their own exquisitely handcrafted opinions on the films. Thus, after a presentation of Robert Altman's *Gosford Park*, a middle-aged woman grandiosely stood up and opined that the film "resembled an impressionist painting."

Expressing such a view was a dicey affair; the impressionists were known for outdoor, sunlit, pastel-colored, intellectually contentless scenes set in nineteenth-century France, whereas Altman's astringent analysis of the class system was set almost entirely indoors in dark, brooding, rainy twentieth-century England. No matter. What it signified was that after so many years of insulation from the lips of the lofty and the perceptions of the perspicacious, I now found myself gazing directly into the eye of the pretentiousness storm.

The *Gosford Park* incident was the first time since I had moved to the suburbs that I no longer felt at home. Now, I am not suggesting that my idea of civilization is a twelve-plex with nine screens showing Adam Sandler films. But consider the alternative. First the Burns Center exhumed the works of Jean Gabin. Then it staged an Eric Rohmer film festival. Most recently it screened Neil Jordan's dreary remake of Jean-Pierre Melville's classic noirish *Bob le Flambeur.* What really irked me at this "séance" was that only three people in the room (seating capacity: 250) had seen the original *Bob le Flambeur*—my wife and I were two of them—suggesting that what we had on our hands here was bargain-basement pretentiousness: faux snobs prepared to carry out the hoity-toity crime without having done the highfalutin time. This was the *coup de grâce,* the *Sturm und Drang,* the *elisir d'amore,* the *je ne sais quoi* and the *sine qua non* all rolled into one. Yes, the vita had been bella. But it was bella no more. Sadly, the time has come to say *auf Wiedersehen, à plus tard, ciao.*

Arctic Circle, here I come.

XIV
FAREWELLS

Good-bye, Old Friend
by Reverend Erik Kolbell

Breaking up may be hard to do, but breaking
off a friendship may be toughest of all.

I meet Ellen at the diner because something's bothering her, and she wants help thinking it through. She sits across the table from me, staring into a half-empty cup, her lips pursed and her brow furrowed, as if she's reading the tea leaves and not at all happy with what they're telling her.

After an awkward silence and with a minimum of coaxing, she launches into a tale of her predicament, which involves an old high-school pal named Carol. As teenagers, they were the best of friends ("Thick as thieves," Ellen says), but now, some ten years later, Ellen notices that their lives have veered in very different directions. Their politics, values, lifestyles, families and interests are less compatible than they once were, and as a result, Ellen is realizing—with equal measures of sadness and guilt—how greatly her energy for maintaining the relationship has ebbed.

As both a practicing psychotherapist and an ordained minister, I had a hunch Ellen was looking to me for two things: advice and permission. Essentially, she wondered if she had a right to end the relationship.

I suspect a great many of us have found ourselves in Ellen's ill-fitting shoes, staring into that same half-empty cup, wanting someone to know that for whatever the reason, the relationship can no longer be as much a part of our lives as it was in the past. The insistent phone calls you avoid returning, the golf invitation you've again deferred, the dinner plans you keep backing out of, each time with slightly less believable excuses. (How often can your littlest one come down with the flu?) And all these dilemmas involve someone you might have once called a good friend. So is it okay to loosen our ties and ratchet down the level of time and attention we give to a friendship? And if so, how do we do it?

First of all, it is okay, because friendships run low on gas for any number of legitimate reasons. In my case, a next-door neighbor who would casually drop in for coffee moved to another town, meaning get-togethers required far more energy than either of us had to give. One of my patient's old college friends was still wearing tie-dyed shirts and listening to the Grateful Dead, while my patient had moved on to Ralph Lauren and Rachmaninoff. For many of us, marriage and children shift our social focus from the singles scene to soccer games and from classes at the Y to conferences at the PTA. And through it all, life becomes more crowded, leaving us with less free time and making it harder for us to choose how, and with whom, we will spend it.

It is indeed healthy to acknowledge that these changes go on, that as human beings we do not simply sit still as life happens to us. We move through it, and inevitably that movement spins us away from people we once held close, people who may still hold us close. And when those people seem to be clinging to the friendship more tightly than we are, they have a right to know how we're feeling and what we're thinking, as tough as it may be for them and for us to face up to that reality.

Thus, when it came time to recap our conversation, Ellen and I identified five major points that any of us would need to address in a situation like Ellen's and that anyone in Carol's position would need to hear.

- Honesty. Avoidance is not only ineffectual, it's the coward's way out. The other person is entitled to an honest admission that your level of commitment to the relationship has changed.

- Inventory. Be in a position to catalogue the reasons this relationship has been so valuable to you over the years.

- Inevitability. Explain that your life's journey has taken you in different directions and that you've drifted away from some of the interests that had come to define this relationship. This is not a judgment, simply an observation; it is the inexorable movement of life.

- Economy. Commiserate over how you both have less time to devote to friendships than they deserve, and say that this makes it difficult but necessary for you to apportion free time more frugally.

- Sadness. Acknowledge that pulling away from the friendship brings a sense of sadness and loss.

Ellen and I then talked about what could be done to make a conversation like this as easy as possible for both parties.

For starters, the conversation should take place somewhere

that ensures uninterrupted privacy and makes the other person feel safe and comfortable. It's helpful to know how to start the conversation, so before you meet, compose an opening sentence that is taut and informative (no beating around the bush) but does not cudgel her with insensitivity: "I know I've been distant lately, and I want to explain to you why I think that's happened."

It's critical that the person who initiates the conversation gives the other party wide latitude to express her feelings, regardless of how painful they may be to hear. Those feelings should be met with compassion but not apology: "I understand why you'd be angry; we've been through a lot together."

Finally, it's equally important to close the conversation by restating the person's importance in your life and reaffirming your hope that the two of you will be able to move on without hard feelings: "I hope we can both get past this; I am so very grateful to you for all you've meant to me over the years."

> We owe it to ourselves and to the other person to be honest without being brutal, to be articulate without sounding scripted.

The benefit of a one-on-one conversation is its immediacy; eye contact, facial expressions and one person's hand placed gently on the other's add to the richness of the communication. A great many sentiments can be expressed without words. Nevertheless, for some of us, all the care and caution in the world might still not make it possible to broach a subject like this face-to-face. In fact, a well-crafted, handwritten letter has its advantages and can incorporate all of what Ellen wants to say to Carol. A letter allows the author time to compose her thoughts and present them to her friend in language that is less likely to be misunderstood, and it allows the reader time and space to digest those thoughts, contemplate them and fashion a reasoned response rather than an impulsive reaction.

Downshifting a friendship is only one of a number of difficult conversations we might need to have with someone we care about. Perhaps we have to ask an in-law not to scold our children or a spouse to do more of the housework. Or perhaps we need to confront a friend about his drinking problem or the money he owes us. Whatever the case may be, we owe it to ourselves and to the other person to be honest without being brutal, to be articulate without sounding scripted, to be calm without seeming indifferent, to be respectful of the other person's views without surrendering to them and to be resolute without being hard-hearted. What makes it difficult to raise certain topics with people we care about is the very fact that we care about them, and when the conversation is over, they should know we still do.

Saying Good-bye Gracefully

by Phyllis Theroux

When remembering the dead, don't forget
the sensibilities of the living.

S ome people view life as a pilgrimage. Others view it as a trip. But no matter what your view, every life consists of a main character moving through a story until it ends—or at least the hands-on portion of it does. Then comes the funeral, when the tale's other characters come together to mourn their loss. Until recently, however, it was rare that detailed stories about the life of the deceased were shared at funeral ceremonies. It used to be that the presider would merely use the occasion to remind mourners that it was time to put their own spiritual houses in order. All of that began to change in the late 1960s, says Monsignor Thomas M. Duffy of the Blessed Sacrament Catholic Church in Washington, D.C. "More people started to speak at funerals after Teddy Kennedy spoke so movingly at the service for his brother Bobby."

"When someone dies," says Rabbi M. Bruce Lustig, the senior rabbi at the Washington Hebrew Congregation, "our relationship with him changes from the physical to the metaphysical. The eulogy is the first opportunity we have to begin that process."

These days it seems that more time than ever is required for speakers to convey their memories to fellow grievers. Often, funerals and memorial services resemble a kind of Last Entertainment, at which mourners are handed programs that include poems and photographs. During the service itself, the deceased is sometimes resurrected in the form of home videos or audio recordings. And frequently there are multiple eulogies. The Right Reverend Jane Holmes Dixon, also of Washington, D.C., believes that the trend has gone too far: "I am concerned that the increased number of eulogies in the rite of Christian burial can sometimes over-shadow the central message of such services: the Resurrection."

In preparing a eulogy, find a quiet place to sit and think. What stories float to the surface?

A good eulogy is a double portrait: of the departed and the eulogist. But when eulogists are left unchecked, the service can really jump the tracks. We all cringe at memories of services at which somebody made a faux pas like reading "Crossing the Bar" as a tribute to an alcoholic or mentioning the deceased's great fondness for gambling. There is also the occa-sional "rogue wave": a former girlfriend who gets up and speaks at length about why she and the deceased decided not to get married, as his widow listens in horror.

The miracle, of course, is that most funerals proceed to the end without incident. Indeed, lives that are fatally flawed or trag-ically brief have often provided a eulogist with powerful sources of inspiration. When the teenage son of a prominent Virginia attorney died in 1993, his father began his eulogy this way: "How do you celebrate a life like John's? How do you celebrate a tragic life and death? How do you find any redeeming value in the life of a retarded boy who suffered from severe and bizarre emotional problems? How do you celebrate a life of dead expectations?"

Many of us have asked ourselves a variation of these questions, and in attempting to answer them for someone whose life is over, the eulogist can help answer them for us all. "John taught us many lessons," said his grieving father. "They have certainly been expensive lessons, and we would never have voluntarily paid this dear price, but the value of these lessons and of John's life is very profound."

Every time I attend a funeral, I am conscious of being in a classroom, trying to learn as much as I can about how to lead the rest of my own life from the life that has just concluded.

When asked to say a few words about somebody who has died, even the most self-confident eulogist can choke. Here is what you must remember:

- In preparing a eulogy, find a quiet place to sit and think. What stories float to the surface? What did you love most about the deceased? What will you miss? Why did he or she make a difference to you? Jot down ideas, scraps of conversation you had. Which thoughts hold the most power? Which words cast the most light?

- Here is what you don't do: talk about yourself. You were chosen because of your close relationship with the deceased. The people in the congregation want to know how you came to enjoy such a position. Just bear in mind that you are the spotlight, not the picture, and you will be on firm ground.

- Remember that a eulogy is not a term paper. At one funeral I attended, the deceased's best friend, who had been with him night and day during his terminal illness, avoided the problem of breaking down in public by instead listing all the legal cases they had worked on together. Everyone knew why he was doing it, but the result was a docket sheet, not a eulogy. You need a few facts to anchor your tribute, but don't hide behind them or your eulogy will seem cold.

- Direct your remarks to the survivors, who are struggling to close the circle newly broken by their friend's death. When I was asked to speak about a young man who had taken his own life, I thought about his peers—all of them of high-school age—who might be worrying that they had pushed him over the precipice by some act of omission or commission. It seemed important to address their fear, so I did.

- It is never acceptable to speak ill of the dead. That's not to say that you can't mention the deceased's struggles. It is how you mention these struggles that makes the difference between shedding light and creating darkness. Ask yourself whether the deceased would cross out any lines of your eulogy if he or she could edit it.

- You are speaking before mourners, not theater critics or CNN cameras. Every kind word or heartfelt thought will be gratefully received.

- Don't be afraid to keep it simple. And while you are preparing your remarks, don't be afraid to grieve. "Sorrow comes in great waves," wrote Henry James. But if you're willing to ride it, sorrow will carry you toward the words you need.

About the Authors

Letitia Baldrige ("The Art of Listening," August 1995) is a writer on manners, and a former social secretary to the White House.

Patricia Beard ("Keeping Your Word," December 1997) former features editor at *Town & Country*, is the author of six books.

Andy Borowitz ("Thank You for Not Sharing," December 2002) is a comedian, actor and writer whose work appears frequently in *The New Yorker*.

Jim Brosseau ("Presume Nothing," April 2005) is a writer, editor and occasional standup comic.

David Brown ("Civility As Our Greatest Defense," November 2001; "Penny-wise, Meet Pound-foolish," May 2003) is an author, film and Broadway producer in New York.

Tom Connor ("Gifts That Go On Giving," December 2003) is a freelance writer in Southport, Connecticut.

Jamie Lee Curtis ("Guess Who's Coming to Dinner?," September 2005) is an award-winning actress and author.

Hugh Downs ("It's Grand *and* Great," June 2004) is a retired anchor for NBC, PBS and ABC-TV Networks.

Karen Duffy ("In the Company of Friends," June 2001) is a writer and TV host in New York City.

Anne Taylor Fleming ("'Whatever' Do You Mean?," September 2003) is a nationally recognized journalist, TV commentator and fiction writer.

Janet Carlson Freed ("How to Treat Your Nanny," June 1998; "To Love and to Cherish?," February 2003) is *Town & Country*'s Director of Beauty and Health.

Sonya Friedman ("Teach Your Daughters Well," November 2002) is a psychologist, author of *Take It From Here* and former CNN host.

Jane Hammerslough ("Material Whirl," January 2005) is the author of more than twenty books.

Philip Herrera ("What I Should Have Said," October 2002), former executive editor of *Town & Country*, is working on a novel set in New York City.

Joan Caraganis Jakobson ("Way Too Familiar?," March 2003) is the author of *And One More Thing: A Mother's Advice on Life, Love, and Lipstick*.

Jill Kargman ("The Return of Gallantry," May 2002; "So What Do You Expect?," June 2003) is co-author of the novels *The Right Address* and *Wolves In Chic Clothing* and lives in New York City.

Erik Kolbell ("Good-bye, Old Friend," April 2003) is a minister and psychotherapist in New York City.

Eileen Livers ("The Subject is Money," February 2004), a writer and editor in New York City, is the author of *The Unofficial Guide to Planning Your Wedding*.

Robert Lopez and **Jeff Marx** ("When Bad Things Happen to Bad People," March 2005) are the composer-creators of the Tony Award-winning Broadway musical *Avenue Q*.

Francine Maroukian ("Let's Make a Meal," November 2003) is a former caterer and the author of *Town & Country Elegant Entertaining*.

Patricia Marx ("Elevator Ups and Downs," October 2004) is a writer whose credits include *Saturday Night Live* and *Rugrats* and books such as *Meet My Staff* and *How To Regain Your Virginity*.

Frank McCourt ("One Hundred Thousand Welcomes," March 2001) is the author of *Angela's Ashes* and *'Tis*.

Peggy Noonan ("What I've Learned," September 2002), a former speechwriter for Ronald Reagan and the senior George Bush, is a columnist, television scriptwriter and author.

Geoffrey Nunberg ("Fighting Words," March 2002) is a linguist at Stanford University and the author of *Going Nuclear*.

Stacey Okun ("Matrimonial Manners," February 2001; "Going Public," May 2001; "Respectful Renting," April 2002) is a contributing editor for *Town & Country* and the author of *Town & Country's Elegant Weddings*.

Charles Osgood ("Win Some, Lose Some," April 2001) is anchor of CBS *Sunday Morning* on television and of the *Osgood File* on CBS Radio.

Christine Pittel ("Kindergarten Madness," November 2000) is a writer and editor in New York City.

Joe Queenan ("The Proliferation of Pretension," July 2003) is a magazine columnist and author of *Queenan Country: A Reluctant Anglophile's Pilgrimage to the Mother Country*.

Andy Rooney ("Playing Our Cards Right," December 2001) is a television essayist and newspaper columnist.

M. J. Ryan ("Have a Little Patience," January 2004) is the author of *The Power of Patience*, among many other books.

John Sedgwick ("Insincerely Yours," October 2001) is the author of three works of nonfiction and two novels; his family memoir, *In My Blood*, will appear in the winter of 2006.

Ted Sorensen ("Patriotic Pride," July 2001), former special counsel to President John F. Kennedy, is a retired New York lawyer.

Anne H. Soukhanov ("Protecting Our Language," September 2001) is U.S. general editor of the *Encarta Webster's Dictionary of the English Language*.

Phyllis Theroux ("Saying Good-bye Gracefully," September 2004) is the author of *The Book of Eulogies*.

Patricia Volk ("Don't Do This in Public," April 2004) is the author of *STUFFED* and a frequent contributor to *The New York Times*.

Martha Woodham ("Stepping Down the Aisle," February 2005) is the author of *The Bride Did What?! Etiquette for the Wedding Impaired* and *Wedding Etiquette for Divorced Families: Tasteful Advice for Planning A Beautiful Wedding*.